16.

D1369550

The Last Days of the Giants?

The Last Days of the Giants?

A Route Map for Big Business Survival

Robert Baldock

JOHN WILEY & SONS, LTD
Chichester • New York • Weinheim • Brisbane • Singapore • Toronto

Copyright © 2000 by John Wiley & Sons Ltd,
Baffins Lane, Chichester,
West Sussex PO19 1UD, England

National   01243 779777
International (+44) 1243 779777
e-mail (for orders and customer service enquiries):
cs-books@wiley.co.uk
Visit our Home Page on http://www.wiley.co.uk
or http://www.wiley.com

Every effort has been made to trace and acknowledge ownership of copyright. The publishers will be glad to hear from any copyright holders whom it has not been possible to contact.

The opinions contained within this book are those of the author and may not accord with those of his past or present employer.

All rights reserved. No part of this publication may be reproduced, stored in a retrieval system, or transmitted, in any form or by any means, electronic, mechanical, photocopying, recording, scanning or otherwise, except under the terms of the Copyright, Designs and Patents Act 1988 or under the terms of a licence issued by the Copyright Licensing Agency, 90 Tottenham Court Road, London W1P 9HE, UK, without the permission in writing of John Wiley and Sons Ltd., Baffins Lane, Chichester, West Sussex, PO19 1UD, UK.

Other Wiley Editorial Offices

John Wiley & Sons, Inc., 605 Third Avenue,
New York, NY 10158-0012, USA

WILEY-VCH Verlag GmbH, Pappelallee 3,
D-69469 Weinheim, Germany

Jacaranda Wiley Ltd, 33 Park Road, Milton,
Queensland 4064, Australia

John Wiley & Sons (Asia) Pte Ltd, Clementi Loop #02-01,
Jin Xing Distripark, Singapore 129809

John Wiley & Sons (Canada) Ltd, 22 Worcester Road,
Rexdale, Ontario M9W 1L1, Canada

Library of Congress Cataloging-in-Publication Data
Baldock, Robert.
   The last days of the giants? : a route-map for big business survival / Robert Baldock.
      p. cm.
   Includes bibliographical references and index.
   ISBN 0-471-72032-X (hardback : alk. paper)
   1. Big business. 2. Corporations. 3. Industries—Social aspects. 4. Industrial management. I. Title.
HB2351.B35 2000
658'.023—dc21   99-053073

British Library Cataloguing in Publication Data
A catalogue record for this book is available from the British Library
ISBN 0-471-72032-1

Typeset in 12 on 16pt Sabon by Mackreth Media Services, Hemel Hempstead
Printed and bound in Great Britain by Biddles Ltd, Guildford and Kings Lynn.
This book is printed on acid-free paper responsibly manufactured from sustainable forestation, for which at least two trees are planted for each one used.

To all of those who have helped me in the past and, I hope, will help me in the future.

Contents

Acknowledgements

THIS, MY SECOND BOOK, SHOULD HAVE BEEN MUCH EASIER than my first. However, as you will see below, fate or, more accurately, ambition intervened.

I applied all of my learnings from the experience of writing my first book. I asked Tim Hindle (who was such a great help on my first book) to help me write the second book since my (demanding) day job still had first call on my time. What I did not reckon on was that somewhere along the way I would decide that it was time for Rob Baldock to pursue his last remaining ambition—to start his own firm. So instead of just having to balance the demands of my firm, family and publisher, I also had to find the time to work out what this new firm of mine would do. Something ultimately had to give and that was the schedule for this book. I had to draw in help from another gifted writer, Neil Baker, as Tim had to start work on another project. That this book eventually saw the light of day was down to the help provided to me by both Tim and Neil and because Wiley, my publishers, were very patient. I thank you all.

I would also like to thank a number of ex-colleagues within Andersen Consulting (they are ex because I have resigned from Andersen Consulting to pursue my ambition) who helped me develop the content and ideas that are at the heart of this book. In particular, I would like to recognise the contributions of Brian Johnson and Jim Marpe. Brian, one of the brightest people I have ever come across, helped me develop the cube that you will read about very soon. Jim, the leader of the Financial Services M&A practice within Andersen Consulting, helped me develop the concise history of the past that you will also read about. Finally, there are two young Andersen people that I would like to recognise—James Tilley and Ronan O'Brien—who did a fantastic job in helping me put the finishing touches to the book.

Enough from me, 'time2' read on. If you are with a giant corporation, take heed. Ignoring the advice in this book could seriously damage your health.

Robert Baldock
December 1999
rob@speed.uk.com

About the Author

ROBERT BALDOCK STARTED THIS BOOK AS A GLOBAL managing partner within Andersen Consulting, responsible for leading Andersen's efforts in eCommerce, Customer Relationship Management and Mergers & Acquisitions within the financial services industry—a $900 million global business. By the time you get to read the book he will, all going well, be the Group Chief Executive of a set of ventures all concerned with helping people save time and improve their quality of life. In other words, he's off to 'solve world hunger'.

Robert joined Andersen Consulting in 1976, in London at the tender age of 21 and became a partner in 1987, thus becoming one of the youngest people ever to make partner in the firm. He also became one of the most frequent travellers in his last few years with the firm, often flying 30,000 miles a month in pursuit of global business opportunities. Whilst this was good news for British Airways, his family thought less of it.

The vast majority of his time with Andersen was spent working in the financial services industry, but he also worked in a whole range of other consuming serving industries helping giant companies and entities from government, health care, retailing, utilities, oil and gas, change for the better.

Within Andersen Consulting he built up a reputation for being a thought leader and innovator; a bit of an 'out-of-the-box' thinker. He was responsible for leading a group of partners in Andersen's global financial services practice in developing a set of scenarios for the future of the financial services industry. The subsequent paper and futuristic video produced as a result of this work—'Virtualisation: The Future of Financial Services'—was highly acclaimed both within and outside of the firm. Shortly afterwards, Robert led another initiative to look at the future shape of the consumer serving industries. This initiative led him to produce his first book—*Destination Z: The History of The Future* (Wiley, 1998)—a book that has been very well received across the globe.

This (second) book was developed from another piece of work that Mr Baldock initiated, to explore what the giant corporations of this world had to do if they were to survive and prosper in the twenty-first century.

He is a regular speaker at conferences, and has written many papers and articles for national and international papers and publications. He will probably pause his book-writing activities as he tries to cope with the demands of running his own business.

He is married to a hugely understanding and talented wife, has two great children, and lives on the outskirts of London. Apart from his family, his main passion is motor racing and cars in general. In what is left of his spare time, he is the Chairman of the UK Motorsport Industry Association, the trade body representing British motorsport.

Executive Summary—
Just when you thought it was
time to relax . . .

T HE WITCHING HOUR HAS PASSED AND IT'S A BRIGHT SUNNY day in the third millennium. Simon Jones, a senior executive with a large corporation, is sitting in his office feeling good about things. He's just got over the Y2K problem without having to call on the emergency services that he'd lined up (just in case), and his finance director has not yet rushed in to tell him that all the millions in the company's bank accounts have been spontaneously switched into thousands.

All's well that ends well, thinks Simon, as he wonders what the pre-millennium fuss was all about. So he opens the bottom drawer of his desk, the place where he keeps a stack of holiday brochures that he promised his partner he'd look at 'once things get a bit quieter'.

Simon is wondering how to choose between the Maldives and the Seychelles when a colleague walks in and gives him a rude awakening.

He tells Simon that an Internet-based firm that he'd never heard of has become his main competitor in Belgium and has stolen the company's most profitable customers—

all within the space of a few months. This news takes Simon by complete surprise. It is, in fact, terrifying. Where did this new competitor come from? Why were they not affected by the millennium freeze? And is it a one-off?

Maybe Bill Gates wasn't speaking just for the benefit of the anti-trust authorities when he said a few years back that Microsoft was always only two years away from failure, thinks Simon. At the time (1997), Microsoft was the 400th largest firm in the world in terms of turnover and the third largest in terms of market capitalisation. If Microsoft was that close, how close am I, he ponders?

Throughout the 1990s he'd had a warm feeling of self-confidence. The riot of mergers and acquisitions that occurred during the decade, and that rose to a crescendo as the century drew to a close, had made it seem that big was beautiful. He could see that the new industries of the information age were throwing up giants just as had the railway, steel and automobile industries before them. Microsoft, Intel and Nokia, all featured in *Fortune* magazine's list of the 500 biggest companies in the world. Big business, he'd believed, is always going to be with us.

Mergers and acquisitions had ploughed ahead at such a rate in the 1990s that the structure of industries right across the board had been transformed. But giants still dominated them. In some sectors, business is concentrated in the hands of a few organisations. In the UK, the top 10 banks and building societies hold 76% of deposit balances. In 1979 Citicorp created a sensation by becoming the first $100 billion bank. In 1999 the three-way merger between Dai-Ichi Kangyo Bank, Fuji Bank and the Industrial Bank of Japan created the first trillion dollar bank ($1,000 billion).

Simon thinks how his friends in the oil industry

remember their youth with nostalgia, a time when there were the 'Seven Sisters', the seven big corporations that then effectively controlled the drilling and distribution of the world's oil and gas. Now the sisters had lost some of their number and much of their charm. A few had died off and others had sought refuge in the homes of the survivors. The remaining sisters were fat and bloated and (something that Simon found particularly disturbing) they were still talking about getting bigger.

He already had a sneaking feeling that the riotous M&A activity may have been brought about not by firms desiring to be bigger because they believed that big was a good thing to be, but rather because they didn't want to be smaller. He realises now, with a searing flash of insight, that once you are big it is extraordinarily painful and complicated to become smaller. There are shareholders and employees whose aspirations can only be satisfied by corporate growth, by insistently regular increases in profit and turnover. So when you are big—and the corporation Simon works for is, by any definition, big—you don't have too many strategic options. In order not to be left behind by everybody else's M&A strategy, others in the 1990s had to do much the same.

Nothing wrong with that, thinks Simon. Change is always with us, and the more practice you can get the better. But his confidence is undermined by a disturbing book he read recently called *The Innovator's Dilemma: When new technologies cause great firms to fail*, (Harvard Business School Press, US, 1997). Written by a Harvard Business School professor, Clayton Christensen, it contains one sentence in particular that made his blood go cold. It is a sentence that sums up the whole book:

There is something about the way that decisions get made in successful organisations that sows the seeds of eventual failure.

Even if you're doing things well . . . or rather, because you're doing things well . . . you may be doomed to fail.

Even before Simon had read the book he'd become increasingly aware that the decision-making process in his large corporation was invariably sticky and slow. Whereas new entrants seemed to be able to take decisions and then implement them in a matter of nanoseconds, his corporation, like other established players, took weeks and even months to put the same type of decision into effect. This was partly the result of trying, over the years, to add checks and balances to 'legacy' systems of decision making rather than having the courage to throw them away and start afresh.

The spate of mergers and acquisitions that had brought his firm to its current size had not been a help either. With each new M&A, the attention of many of the organisation's most senior managers had been diverted to internal affairs, to the reallocation of jobs, functions and fixed assets. That had taken their eyes off the external market and allowed undistracted newcomers to gain a critical advantage.

Moreover these undistracted newcomers seemed to be playing the game almost by a different set of economic rules. Their strategy was focused on getting themselves a high stock market quotation in double quick time by means of an Initial Public Offering (IPO). To do this they built up an impressive client list by pricing their work at more-or-less cost—a price Simon cannot hope to match because his costs are 100 times higher. That pricing strategy increased their turnover very rapidly, but not their profit. The market, however, seemed not to be too fussed about profit. A long string of Internet start-ups, for example, were valued at the time of their IPOs in the late 1990s at several billion dollars. And that was before a single cent had appeared on their bottom line.

This strategy had allowed the newcomers to attract half-a-dozen top people with a promise of equity when the company went public. Many of these people became hugely wealthy after the IPO, in much shorter time than it would have taken them to become a director or a partner of a more traditional organisation.

And then the final agony. When these newcomers found that things were not going their way they were able to 'morph' into something else with electrifying speed. Unlike Simon, they were not stuck with the shape of failure for more than an instant.

Help, he cries, as he forgets about the break in the Maldives. How on earth is his firm going to survive in this environment? Is there any hope of a rosy future for big business in general? Well, never mind 'in general'. He just focuses on the particular. Is there any hope of a rosy future for his big business in particular?

A new era

In this book I argue that much of the environment in which the culture of 'bigness' blossomed is fast disappearing in many industries. There is a seismic shift in the industrial cost structure demonstrated by the nifty little newcomers heading single-mindedly for their IPO.

There is also a shift in the industrial power structure,

in the influence that different groups of stakeholders bring to bear on production and the processes involved in it. For a start, we are entering a buyer-driven era, an era in which the customer will not just be a king but a dictator! And the great power of organised unions and centralised government, which dominated the industrial scene for much of the twentieth century, is rapidly being diffused.

These and other dramatic changes in the industrial environment are undermining the competitive advantages that traditional large corporations have enjoyed for the best part of a century. Does this spell the end for these large corporations? Will they become the dinosaurs of the twenty-first century?

I believe that there is life after the age of the giants. But in order to enjoy it, the large traditional organisations of today will have to become very different.

The process of transformation will not be easy, and only a few of today's giants will survive. But I believe that there is a way for them to follow if they want to thrive in this new business environment . . . if they think of their future as moving along three different dimensions.

Giants rule, OK?

In the first chapter I set the scene by describing the recent history of large corporations. The twentieth century has, by and large, been dominated by them. The economics and politics of business throughout the period have favoured size over and above suppleness and agility.

The picture has been slightly confused by the fact that there are at least four different measures of corporate size in common use: turnover, total assets, employees and market capitalisation. A company that is large by one of these yardsticks is not necessarily large by all the others. There are companies (like commodity traders for instance) which have huge turnovers and very small numbers of employees.

The size culture has been driven first and foremost by the assembly-line techniques developed in the early years of the twentieth century. These enabled manufacturers to reap huge economies of scale and thereby to reach a mass market with products and services that had previously been the preserve of the wealthy.

In addition, throughout the century, corporate life was dominated by stakeholders who had a great interest in ensuring that corporations remain large. For the most part, governments, workers and managers preferred large corporations.

Although governments ostensibly fought against excessive concentrations of industrial power with various forms of anti-trust legislation, there was a tendency for right-wing governments to favour large corporations because they were frequently their major source of funding. Left-wing governments also favoured large corporations because the trade unions (on whom they relied for their funding) also preferred them. For powerful trade unions and their worker-members, large corporations gave surer guarantees of continuing jobs.

Managers inside corporations also tended to look for greater size. It massaged their egos and (more importantly) it opened opportunities for them to reduce competition. As Adam Smith pointed out in *The Wealth of Nations* (*First published 1776*. Prometheus Books, 1991), his classic economic treatise written in 1776:

People of the same trade seldom meet together, even for merriment and diversion, but the conversation ends in a conspiracy against the public, or in some contrivance to raise prices.

Then there was the fact that larger companies had easier access to finance. In the UK this phenomenon was originally called the Macmillan Gap—after the chairman of the committee which first identified it in 1931. As late as 1980 the Wilson Committee (another group charged with looking into the UK's financial system) reported that:

Compared to large firms, small firms are at a considerable disadvantage in financial markets.

The groups who gained least from the corporate tendency to gigantism were ordinary shareholders and consumers. It is only in recent years, as the power of these two groups has grown, that the balance in favour of greater size has begun to be redressed.

Over the years, companies have grown in three different ways, but for the larger part of the century only two of these options were, in reality, open to them. The first option was to grow through organic growth, through the normal market mechanisms of producing and selling more and more, year in, year out. The second option was to grow through merger or acquisition (M&A), by buying or merging with another existing corporation.

Throughout industrial history, there has been a tendency for M&A activity to go in cycles. There was a rash of it in the 1880s in the US oil and steel industries, in the 1920s in the UK chemicals industry (resulting in the formation of ICI, Imperial Chemical Industries), and then again in the late 1990s.

By the time of the most recent rash, corporations had developed a third option for growth. This was through the formation of strategic alliances with each other. Strategic alliances differ from the standard corporate alliance, which is merely an extension of a firm's contractual arrangements. They necessarily involve some sort of sharing of risks and rewards between 'the allies', and they mark a fundamental shift in the way in which corporations are able to satisfy their need for growth.

These three varieties of growth can be termed, 'Build, Buy and Ally'. Many firms resort to the last two because the first is too slow. And increasingly they resort to the third because the second often fails to deliver improved competitiveness.

The threat to the giants

In the second chapter of the book, I describe the forces that are working against industrial gigantism today. Among the most significant are:

1. **The arrival of new, Internet-based firms that are more agile and innovative than the giants.** The Internet is helping to put small agile newcomers on a par with large corporations and able to compete head on with them for new business. Just as Microsoft could appear from virtually nowhere to usurp the market of mighty IBM, so a few years later Netscape appeared overnight and threatened to undermine the market (and the size) of

Microsoft. Who will be next? And where will they come from? In this world, small agile firms have an advantage over giant organisations that are unable to take decisions quickly. This process will accelerate as more and more companies join the eCommerce bandwagon.

2.   **A shift in power from the seller to the buyer.** The convergence of computing, communications and content in the shape of personal computers (PCs) hooked up over a network to the Internet has triggered a revolution in the way business is conducted. Users of these technologies have 24-hour access to almost everything, everywhere. Internet-based search agents make it possible for these users to track down the cheapest products in seconds, and new Internet-based intermediaries (the so-called 'infomediaries') have created a new form of commerce whereby the buyer sets the price, not the seller.

3.   **Changing government attitudes towards the giants.** Governments have become less enchanted with big business. They have stopped mergers from going ahead and have sought to break up some of the larger firms to create more competition. Through a programme of deregulation they have also forced the large incumbents to focus more on the needs of their customers and to drop their prices.

4.   **Industry convergence.** Many large companies are moving into new markets (e.g. retailers into financial services). They are doing this for one of two reasons: either because their own markets give them little scope for growth; or as part of a drive

to hang onto their most profitable customers by offering them a broader range of products and services. In both cases, these assaults on new markets are being made with new products or services at incredibly low prices.

5. **A very short-term focus.** Institutional investors and brokers' analysts have become very demanding of public companies. In the United States in particular, they relentlessly demand an improvement in results every quarter. Fail to deliver against this expectation, and top managers are out, regardless of their past track record (as happened in the case of Eckhard Pfeiffer, the ex-CEO of Compaq). Against this backdrop, companies have become reluctant to make large, long-term investments for fear of damaging their short-term results.

These five forces have led to the most competitive environment in the history of commerce, and they spell big trouble for the giants which may have become too big to respond quickly to the threats that they pose.

Three-dimensional survival

If big firms are going to thrive in this intensely competitive environment, they are going to have to radically alter the way they do things in three different areas or dimensions (See Figure E1):

1. The nature of what they offer to their customers.
2. The nature of the relationship they have with their customers.

3. Their level of virtualisation—i.e. the extent to which a firm tries to do everything itself, or works with third parties to deliver the same (or an increased) scope of service.

In Chapter 3 I briefly describe the three main dimensions listed above.

The first dimension is the nature of what's on offer to consumers in the marketplace. Today most firms sell the traditional type of products that we all know and love (such as basic foodstuffs). Increasingly these same firms are selling 'solutions' which address the underlying consumer need (e.g. for a hot enjoyable meal).

Beyond solutions, but along the same axis, lies something that we call 'Intentions'. An Intention is a desire or goal that may take a person many years to achieve and may involve the integration of products and solutions from multiple firms spanning multiple industries. For example, 'Having an enjoyable retirement' could involve a move to a sunny climate, a new hobby, making financial provisions for your nearest and dearest, and so on.

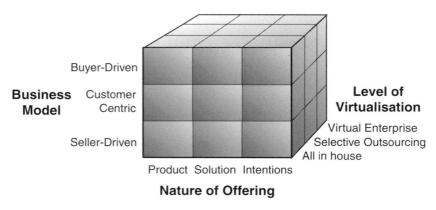

Figure E1   The cube route to success

As a firm moves further along this axis it will find it easier to differentiate its offerings from the competition's. At the same time, customers will find it harder to rely on price alone to assess the value of its products and services.

Along the second axis lie changes in the business model, in the way that sellers and buyers relate to each other. Here we start from a situation where markets are seller-driven. Today, sellers presume to know what the market might want to buy. But we are moving to a much more customer-centric world, a world where sellers will try to tailor their products to meet fast-changing consumer needs.

Beyond the customer-centric world lie buyer-driven markets, markets where the customer dictates what he or she wants, and where producers scurry and scramble to provide it. In such a world, consumers will provide trusted intermediaries with personal details about themselves and their needs. And these intermediaries will invite producers to bid for the business. In such a market there is no room for producers to draw conclusions in advance about what customers might want.

Finally, along the third axis lies the level of virtualisation of the enterprise itself. On this axis we start from a situation where firms attempt to do everything in-house (although there are always notable exceptions, like the advertising function). From here we move on to a situation where firms are selective about those processes in their business which they carry out themselves and those which they outsource to others.

Beyond this outsourcing model lies the virtual enterprise—the enterprise which carries out very few processes itself, but which can nevertheless organise others to produce products of substantial size and complexity. In a previous book (*Destination Z: The History of the Future*) I postulated what I called Baldock's Law. It stated that:

A virtual enterprise has a 1% market share per employee.

I believe that we will see more and more companies formed that satisfy my law.

The three dimensions described above make up the cube that is the icon for this book. Along each dimension there are three steps as described above, so there are (as it were) 27 'cubelets' that make up the larger cube.

The general direction of change is from the bottom, left-hand corner (which is where most firms are today) towards the top, right-hand corner.

The next three chapters go on to describe the three dimensions in more detail.

Dimension One— Changing offerings

In Chapter 4 I focus on the first dimension of the cube—the change in what's on offer in the market and the shift from products, through solutions and on to intentions.

Consumers will become increasingly dissatisfied with traditional goods designed and mass produced by corporations that think they know what people want to buy. Time is running out for plain vanilla products that sit on shelves waiting for people to happen along and buy them.

To respond, organisations will have to know far more about customers so that they can offer products and services that they will buy because they are solutions to their problems. They will have to take their products and services to the customer, when in the past the customer came to them. Direct selling of goods and services around the clock provides a solution to a problem experienced by many consumers—'How can I get to a shop when it is open and when I have free time?'

Dimension Two—
The customer as dictator

In Chapter 5 I describe in some detail the second dimension of the cube—the shift from a seller-driven market to a buyer-driven market, via a customer-centric intermediate stage. Arguably this is the dimension of change that is the most radical and that has the widest implications for business in the future.

Today, consumers are only able to buy what a business wants to make available. But in the buyer-driven market of tomorrow, the tables will be turned and customers will tell businesses what to produce. New technologies will enable them to state, 'This is what *I* want, and these are *my* terms and conditions. Supply me if you wish'. In such a world the location of the customer becomes the location of the business—be it on a phone or on a beach.

The intermediate stage, where the pressure is to become more customer-centric, companies become much more sensitive to ways in which they can meet their customers' needs. This stage can be seen already in a number of businesses. Amazon.com, for example, the Internet-based bookseller, is building up a profile of each of its customers through the books that they order and the way in which they respond to various electronic dialogues. This enables the company to focus its marketing efforts for new titles onto the narrow band of people most likely to be interested.

Ultimately, in the buyer-driven market, consumers will set up their own Web sites on which they will advertise their individual requirements and needs. Firms will then bid to satisfy these needs. Such sites will become living, breathing things that change continually. Andersen Consulting has developed a prototype of such a site. Called mySite!, it literally takes care of a lot of the more mundane tasks, acting, like a personal butler.

Dimension Three— Stop doing everything

In Chapter 6 I describe in detail the third dimension of change, the organisational switch whereby firms that predominantly did everything in-house (and for themselves) decide instead to outsource almost all their operations and processes. *In extremis*, such firms become virtual organisations.

'The day when a single company could operate autonomously in a single industry is long gone', wrote C. Rudy Puryear, my ex-colleague at Andersen Consulting, in a recent edition of *Outlook*, the Andersen Consulting magazine. Firms are increasingly interlinked with each other, and many of them are linked through outsourcing agreements which pass the responsibility for processes (and sometimes for whole operations) of the firm to other businesses.

Many firms have already travelled a long way in this direction and are now committed to selective outsourcing and the formation of wide networks of strategic alliances with other companies.

The journeys ahead

In Chapter 7, I examine the paths forward for the giants of today. What course can they take through the Cube so that they emerge at the other end as living, successful organisations?

There are many ways for them to move forward within the three dimensions of the cube. The only thing they cannot do is to stand still. But some paths through the cube will prove to be dead ends, and from these there will be no turning back.

By and large, however, their journey through the Cube will involve three stages, and these we have called Triage, Integrate and Buyerise. In the first stage, firms will have to reassess the economics of their sales and delivery channels. They will have to focus on customer profitability and sort out their customers according to their quality and value.

In the second stage (Integrate) firms will need to move to a more customer-centric business model in which products and distribution channels are more closely integrated so that they cut across the functional 'silos' of the old-fashioned firm.

Finally, firms will move into a third stage (Buyerise) in which they will turn their business model through 180 degrees in order to come up with value-creating packages that satisfy consumers' intentions.

Whatever journey a firm takes, the giants of today will

inevitably go through a painful sliming process. But how much weight will they lose, and where? And will they be able to slim down gradually over time, or will there need to be some drastic dieting?

1

Giants Rule, OK?

The industrial history of the twentieth century is a story of the triumph of size. It is the century in which 'mass production' was invented (by the Ford Motor Company in 1913), and the century in which rapid economic growth produced markets whose size allowed companies to benefit from huge economies of scale and of scope. If there was a time during those hundred years when it was beautiful to be small, it was completely overshadowed by the time when it was more fashionable to be big.

One economist even came up with a law to prove that big was inevitable. Gibrat's Law of Proportionate Effect is named after Robert Gibrat, a Frenchman who in the 1930s expounded a theory based on his empirical observation that large, medium and small firms grow, on average, by the same proportionate amount.

In 1998 General Motors' (GM) turnover was $161 billion. A 1% increase in this turnover would be $1.6 billion, enough to buy several, sizeable dealerships, while a 1% increase in the turnover of a large GM dealership would amount to $1.6 million, say. Thus, while the big get a lot bigger, says Gibrat's Law, the small only get a bit bigger. Hence, over time, big corporations are continually stretching the distance between themselves and their small and medium-sized rivals.

The extent to which the world has changed since Gibrat's time can be gauged from the way in which his basic premise has been undermined. Small and medium-sized firms may grow on average at the same rate as large firms, but today there are an awful lot of them that grow an awful lot faster. Both IBM and Microsoft, for example, were small companies at one time not so long ago.

Types of growth

Behind the new generation of what one might call 'large-small companies', i.e. those that by some of the traditional measures are undeniably big yet continue to behave as if they were small, is a shift in the nature of corporate growth. Virgin, for example, gives the appearance of being one big firm but is actually several separate firms overseen by a small number of people who work out of the house of its founder, Richard Branson. Companies nowadays are seeking to grow in a different way from the ways that they traditionally grew in the twentieth century.

There are basically only three types of corporate growth:

+ *organic:* through the firm's own efforts and an increase in its sales;
+ *mergers and acquisitions* (M&A): through buying another company and adding the two firms together; and
+ *strategic alliances:* through forming a network connecting a number of organisations in a way that enables them to leverage their ability to increase their business.

These three types of growth I call, 'Build, Buy and Ally'. Over time, firms have used different combinations of the three, depending on the state of their industry and of the economy. But, in general, the early twentieth century was a time of building, and the late twentieth century was a time of buying. The twenty-first century will, by necessity, be a time for allying.

Build

For most companies, the prime time for organic growth is in their early years. When a firm first finds a new and growing market, its energies are focused internally, on things like production. It tends not to look much outside itself.

In the early years of the twentieth century, corporate growth occurred organically in young growing industries such as automobiles and electrical goods. Companies grew as their markets grew. General Electric, for example, grew on average by 9.9% per annum between 1900 and 1930. Mergers between firms in these industries were rare.

The automobile industry also enjoyed a long period of growth after the Second World War and mergers between firms were again infrequent. In the late 1990s, however, sluggish growth pushed a number of companies into each other's arms. Daimler-Benz and Chrysler merged in an unprecedented demonstration of German-American industrial togetherness, and Ford took over Volvo.

Many service industries also enjoyed long periods of organic growth after the Second World War. Real estate and financial services, for example, increased their share of American output from 8.2% and 2.7%, respectively in

1950 to 11.7% and 6.1% in 1990 (US GDP grew by a factor of 20 during this period). But the spate of mergers in the financial services industry at the end of the 1990s suggested that this industry too might finally have run out of organic steam.

A study by Andersen Consulting of the reasons why organic growth was poor among financial services firms in the mid-to-late 1990s found the main culprit to be ineffective and inefficient marketing and sales delivery. Firms simply found it more cost-effective to buy customers on Wall Street than to attract them on Main Street. For a sample of US commercial banks that had above-average revenue growth and that were among the top one-third in shareholder returns over the period 1992 to 1997, nearly 90% of their revenue growth was attributable to M&A.

In theory, the use of improved marketing methods (direct mail, telemarketing and even marketing via the Internet) should give a new zest to traditional companies' attempts to bolster their rates of organic growth. Some of the high hopes that executives have had for direct marketing techniques, however, seem likely to prove elusive.

Buy

For companies in a hurry, mergers and acquisitions are an alternative to organic growth. M&A is also an alternative favoured by laggards. Industries where the rate of sales growth lags behind the average tend to be merger-intensive. Large firms also are more prone to mergers than smaller firms.

This was true even before the twentieth century began. At the end of the nineteenth century there was a number of large mergers in the UK in industries such as textiles, brewing and cement—industries that even by that time were mature. Then there was another wave of mergers in the 1920s, concentrating this time on the rapidly maturing chemicals industry in particular.

There has been nothing, however, to compare with the M&A phenomenon of the last two decades of the twentieth century. Throughout the 1970s the number of mergers and acquisitions by the 1,000 largest companies in Europe (a not atypical sample) remained fairly constant at just over 100 each year. But the number then increased rapidly, shooting up from 275 in 1984/85 to 830 in 1989/90.

There was a slight hiccup during the recession of the early 1990s, but M&A activity surged to all-time record levels in the last years of the century. According to figures compiled by Securities Data Company, the total number of mergers and acquisitions around the world in 1990 amounted to 11,300. By 1994 that figure had risen to 19,300 and by 1998 to 26,200.

The rise in the value of deals was even more astounding. Securities Data Company reckons that the value of all mergers and acquisitions worldwide rose from less than $500 billion in 1993 to almost $2.5 trillion in 1998. Even in Asia, where the devaluation of the Thai baht in July 1997 sparked off an economic crisis across the region, there was little slowing down in the level of activity. The number of deals in Asia (other than Japan) was slightly less in both 1997 and 1998 than in 1996, but the value of M&A in the two latter years was higher (by far) than ever before.

The second quarter of 1998 was the most remarkable three-month period ever recorded in the history of M&A.

In that time eight of the ten largest mergers and acquisitions ever to have taken place were announced. Of the eight, four were in financial services.

Deals such as these propelled firms to enormous size. At the end of 1998 the total assets of the Citigroup financial services empire amounted to $669 billion. At the beginning of the 1990s the largest bank in the world (Dai-Ichi Kangyo Bank) had assets of 'only' $408 billion.

The more time passed, however, the more evidence appeared to prove that mergers and acquisitions rarely worked. In deal after deal it became apparent that shareholders would have been better off if the deal had never taken place. Managers became frustrated with the great difficulty of making mergers add value, and they increasingly began to look for a 'third way' to grow, or at least to strengthen their position.

Ally

The third way that they found was via strategic alliances, a term that embraces a range of formal and informal agreements between firms which commit them to working together for a specific purpose, and to sharing the risks and rewards. (See Figure 1.1 for the range of options for a strategic alliance.) The purpose may be the management of the firm's information technology or the supply of its raw materials and services. There are few rules about who makes a suitable ally. On occasions, alliances have been formed between firms that are in most respects direct competitors.

The number of alliances entered into by major firms has been growing exponentially in recent years. Firms such

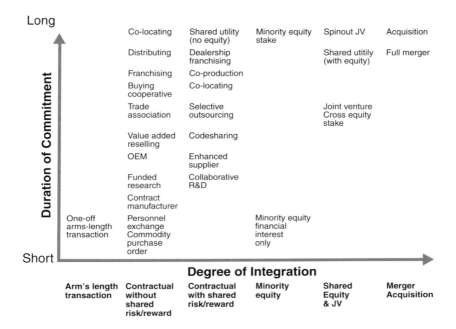

Figure 1.1   Alliance definition: the range of options

as IBM, AT&T, Hewlett Packard and General Motors set up hundreds of different alliances in the 1990s. So rapidly have these networks of alliances grown that many firms' executives are not aware of how large and significant they have become. In a recent survey of over 300 senior executives, Andersen Consulting found that they dramatically underestimated the extent of their organisations' network.

Charles Roussel, director of Andersen Consulting's Mergers, Acquisitions and Alliances Centre of Excellence, drew some conclusions from the findings of this survey:

"A new model for the global organisation is emerging. It is based on a complex set of business relationships that stretch beyond the boundaries of any single enterprise. Technology

webs, economic webs and product webs have already redirected the computer and communications industries, and are threatening to overtake financial services, pharmaceuticals and even chemicals. DuPont's intention to create a virtual conglomerate is a case in point.

Yet alliances are a difficult proposition. They are expensive, requiring modifications to information systems, equipment and facilities. They are invasive, requiring outsiders to wander the halls and inspect one's brains. They are threatening, introducing a greater degree of interdependence with which few feel comfortable. And they are economically risky, as timely integration (most often conducted under intense market scrutiny) becomes geometrically more complex and difficult once more than two parties are involved."

Alliances are, however, a great way for companies to go for a 'test drive', to try out a new business or a new market. For traditional firms, they present a way for them to join in with the dynamic new small entrepreneurial businesses that are being created out of the rise of Net-centric technology and customer-centric markets. When organic growth is too slow, and M&A too unsuccessful, strategic alliances are the promising alternative.

The meaning of big

Growth through strategic alliances is not properly measurable in traditional ways. In the past, the definition of corporate size was never straightforward. But a large company was a bit like a zebra: it might be hard to define but there was no mistaking it when you saw it. Today that is not the case. Through their networks of strategic alliances, companies can have great power and leverage and yet still seem small by traditional measures.

The most commonly used traditional measure of corporate size is turnover and this, fundamentally, is the measure used by *Fortune* magazine. The Fortune 500 is the most famous and authoritative listing of large companies in the world.

For a number of industries, however, turnover is a misleading indicator. For a bank, for example, interest income is probably the closest proxy for turnover. But interest income is not so much a measure of the size of the bank's business as of the general level of interest rates in an economy at a particular time, a level that is heavily influenced by government policy and by rates of inflation.

For this reason, banks are usually ranked according to the size of their balance sheet—how many deposits and loans they have on their books. But this measure is again unsatisfactory because it invalidates any comparison between commercial banks (which lend money that appears on their balance sheets) and investment banks (which lend money which comes from other people's balance sheets). In terms of the amount of business done (i.e. the money lent), investment banks may well be far bigger than seemingly much larger commercial banks.

Turnover is also a misleading measure of the size of trading companies, firms whose *raison d'être* is to buy and sell vast quantities of merchandise at very low margins. Charles Schwab's online brokerage service, for instance, processed, on average, $2 billion of trades per day in 1998. Yet the firm employs only 1,800 people.

Another measure of size, market capitalisation, gets round many of the problems with turnover, and provides a basis for comparing the size of companies in one industry with those in another. Market capitalisation, however, also has its shortcomings. It does not provide a measure of those large firms that are not quoted on a stock exchange. And it is hugely sensitive to the whims of the market.

For the purposes of this book we do not need a very precise definition of what it is to be a large company. In general, in the twentieth century large companies employed tens of thousands of people and sold billions of dollars-worth of goods every year. Unless the company was a bank, that is, in which case it had to have assets of tens of billions of dollars. Suffice it to say that in the twenty-first century such measures of size will become increasingly meaningless.

The advantages of size

Companies have sought to grow their profits, sales, balance sheets, etc. because there have been some very distinct advantages attached to scale in the twentieth century. In the first instance, it has appeared to offer the promise of suppressing competition.

Adam Smith made the point (and almost every industrial economist since has agreed with him) that given a choice between more competition and less competition, 99.5 businessmen out of every 100 will choose to have less. That was as true of the Rockerfellers and the Du Ponts over 100 years ago as it is of Bill Gates and Richard Branson today.

Size in itself does not suppress competition. For many years the giant organisations Procter & Gamble and

Unilever have between them controlled a remarkable share of the markets for various washing products. Yet the two firms are fiercely competitive and there is little evidence that consumers have done anything but benefit from the level of concentration (i.e. the percentage of a nation's industry that is in the hands of its largest firms) in their markets.

But although size may not be a sufficient condition for suppressing competition, it is certainly a necessary one. Small firms are almost invariably at the mercy of rivals with larger market shares. Hence the decision by many firms to follow the example of one of the most influential business leaders of the last quarter of the twentieth century. Jack Welch, the chairman of General Electric, has vowed to take his firm out of any market in which he is not the leader, or among the first two or three.

What size has enabled firms to do over the years is to form cartels among themselves more easily. Those cartels have then set out to fix prices or production levels, and thereby to reduce competition. In the years between the two world wars, international cartels were found in many major industries—oil, steel, chemicals and aluminium, to name but a few. Several of these were negotiated between national market leaders in different industries. This was partly because nationalism in a number of major economies precluded international expansion for many firms.

The oil industry, continually dominated by large firms, has always been susceptible to cartels. In 1928, long before OPEC (the Organisation of Petroleum Exporting Countries) set up the most notorious cartel of recent times, the three largest oil companies in the world, Shell, British Petroleum (then called Anglo-Persian) and Standard Oil of New Jersey, forged an agreement in which they pledged to combine their non-US interests and to share each other's production facilities. This was not unusual for the time.

Cartels were a mutually beneficial way of ensuring that each of the national market leaders in an industry kept their home patch to themselves and did not undermine their margins by competing with each other on foreign turf. At the same time they allowed each firm to aim for global dominance of its markets—the ultimate goal of many a power-hungry twentieth-century chief executive.

The chairman of ICI, for one. In a notorious confidential memo written in 1926 by an official of Du Pont, an American chemicals company, after a conversation with Sir Harry (later Lord) McGowan, the British chairman of the then recently formed Imperial Chemical Industries (ICI), the author wrote:

> "Sir Harry . . . went on to give me a general picture of what he . . . had in mind in the matter of international agreements . . . Sir Harry explained that the formation of ICI is only the first step in a comprehensive scheme which he has in mind to rationalise the chemical manufacture of the world. The details of the scheme are not worked out, not even in Sir Harry's own mind, but the broad picture includes working arrangements between three groups—the IG in Germany, Imperial Chemical Industries in the British Empire, and Du-Ponts and Allied Chemical and Dye in America. The next step in the scheme is an arrangement of some sort between the Germans and the British."

This was written eight years after the end of one war between Britain and Germany and 13 years before the next!

Gaining economies of scale

The search for economies of scale has been another powerful spur to the growth of firms in the twentieth century. Economies of scale—things which cause the average cost of producing an item to fall as the volume of its output increases—can be of two types:

1. *Internal*—cost savings which accrue to a firm regardless of the industry, market or environment in which it operates.
2. *External*—cost savings which accrue to a firm from the way in which its industry is organised.

Internal economies arise in a number of areas. For example, it is easier for large firms to carry the overheads of sophisticated research and development (R&D). To an industry like pharmaceuticals, R&D is absolutely vital. Yet the cost of 'discovering' the next blockbuster drug is enormous, and increasing. Merck, the largest drugs company in the world (by prescription sales), spends some $1.68 billion a year on R&D. Several of the mergers between pharmaceuticals companies in recent years have been driven by little more than the firms' desire to spread their R&D expenditure across a greater volume of sales.

Internal economies can also be gained from spreading the high fixed costs of plant and machinery across a larger volume of sales. Electric power generation and steel manufacturing are two industries where a sizeable critical mass of turnover is required before an initial capital investment in plant and machinery can be justified. They are not businesses for the faint hearted.

Large firms also gain internal economies of scale from the fact that they are able to use specialised labour and machinery more efficiently than small firms. A big firm's complicated assembly line and its specialist workers are less likely to be left expensively idle than those of a small firm.

The cluster factor

External economies of scale are those things that explain why industries tend to cluster round each other—why, for instance, large cities tend to have a financial 'district' where banks and other financial institutions choose to be close neighbours.

Examples of clustering exist in other industries too—most of the UK's national newspapers used to be published in Fleet Street, and the street's name is still used to refer to the industry as a whole. London's diamond dealers are clustered in Hatton Garden, and the glassblowers of Venice are huddled together on the island of Murano to which they were banished centuries ago when their furnaces became too threatening to the great palaces of the Grand Canal.

But it is not just timeworn businesses that in the days before the internal combustion engine needed to be within walking distance of each other that cluster in this way. If it were, then why are all the major US car manufacturers in Detroit? And how come such a big percentage of America's most important computer firms grew out of one small valley in California, a valley now known universally as Silicon Valley?

Even today's most ultra-modern Internet firms have a

tendency to cluster in just a few locations. And they are supposed to be the pioneers of the first industry to be freed from all constraints of time and space.

The fact is that firms gain several benefits from being physically close to each other. For example, their proximity can lead to the development of nearby ancillary services, which they can then all share. Car-parts producers have set up near the small number of major manufacturers, for instance, and can service them, to the mutual benefit of all. The high-precision engineers required by today's fiercely competitive Formula One motor-racing teams have also chosen to cluster together, in their case in the English Midlands.

Modern high-tech clusters have often gathered around prestigious universities on whose research they hope to piggyback. Silicon Valley is near Stanford University, and there are similar high-tech clusters around Harvard University near Boston, and around Cambridge University in the UK.

In some cases, those ancillary services that have been set up to service industrial clusters have remained *in situ* and developed into vibrant new industries long after their original client industry has faded. In the UK, for instance, the leather workers of Somerset, laid off by the decline in the local shoe industry, have diverted their labour into several small but up-market, high value-added leather-goods manufacturers. This has given these highly skilled workers a chance to stay in the region where they have their roots. It also enables them to move more easily to other employers if necessary, and they can probably find the tools of their trade more rapidly in the locality than anywhere else.

Economies of scope

Economies of scale come from doing one thing on an ever-bigger scale. But companies also discovered in the twentieth century that there are economies to be made from doing more and more things on a relatively modest scale. These are called economies of scope, and they provided another reason for companies to get bigger.

This time growth comes not through consolidation of existing businesses but through diversification—through adding new businesses onto those that firms already do, and then making savings by selling a wider range of goods with the same infrastructure. If department stores can profitably sell everything from armchairs to underwear, the argument goes, then why can't tobacco companies also 'make' insurance and oil products? An example of such a company that has diversified in this way is BAT who have moved into completely unrelated markets such as financial products and Formula 1 motor racing (with their BAR team).

Economies of scope were the driving force behind the growth of vast international conglomerates in the 1970s and 1980s, for example companies like BTR and Hanson in the UK and America's ITT. ITT simultaneously owned bakeries, telephone companies, hotels and a forest-products business. In the early 1970s it had over 400 separate subsidiaries operating in over 70 different countries.

Hanson was a classic example of a company that grew through diversification. In the early 1960s it was a small family trucking business based in Yorkshire. By the early 1990s its eponymous chairman, Lord Hanson, had turned it into Britain's fourth largest manufacturer through a series of bold mergers and acquisitions, both in the UK and the USA.

The bold moves began, as they did for many British firms that grew rapidly at the same time (Polly Peck and the advertising group WPP, for instance) with the purchase of a small unknown quoted company. In 1969 Hanson and his partner Gordon White bought a small quoted company called Wiles. They changed its name to Hanson Trust and used it as a vehicle to raise money on the stock market and to buy ever-larger businesses.

Hanson Trust ended up at one time making batteries, typewriters, bricks, HP sauce and Jacuzzi whirlpool baths in a riot of diversification that had little industrial logic behind it. It had a financial logic to it, however.

It worked like this: in 1983 the company paid £255 million for a relatively drab business called United Draperies. It immediately recovered £185 million of the purchase price by the astute sale of bits of the group. The extra profits helped it to raise more money and to make more purchases. By the end of the decade it was buying companies that cost it billions of pounds.

Its growth, however, depended on being able to add shareholder value by making bigger and bigger acquisitions. As with much other industrial diversification, there turned out to be little synergy to be gained from making batteries and bricks under one roof. In the end, the only economies of scope came from sharing a narrow range of head office skills and a chief executive. Many of those skills were focused on making acquisitions.

By the 1990s industrial conglomerates of this sort had gone out of favour, and there were fewer and fewer candidates for the Hanson treatment. Once the group failed in its 1991 bid to take over ICI, the writing was on the wall. By the end of the decade the many different parts of

Hanson had been dramatically unbundled. From being a company worth $13.4 billion at the beginning of the 1990s it was worth 'only' $4.9 billion in 1997, which for Hanson, represented quite a 'shrinkage'. Over the period, BTR and ITT underwent similar downsizing.

In the late 1990s, however, the search for economies of scope reappeared in a new guise. A number of conglomerates were put together in a burst of enthusiasm for cross selling. Companies like the American group Cendant excited the stock market with the promise of synergies to come from (in its case) selling hotel rooms, insurance and car-rentals from under one roof. And the massive combination of Travelers Group and Citicorp in 1998 was driven by the expectation of big cost savings and increased revenues as the sales team of one cross-sold the financial products of the other.

The growth of mass markets

Economies of scale and of scope were the Holy Grail of twentieth-century industrialists. Pursuit of these economies lay behind the creation of mass markets and the emergence of the 'consumer society'.

Their impact is well demonstrated by the history of the car industry. When the motor car was first manufactured it was a rich man's toy. Designed as a luxury product, its wealthy purchasers were not expected to drive it themselves. It was assumed that they would always sit in the back, and the back seat therefore was the main selling point. It had ample legroom, and it was kitted out with little luxuries (like 'vanity cases') to attract a buyer's wife.

It did not matter that the car was technically

complicated and difficult to drive. That was not the concern of the purchaser/owner because he, it was always assumed, would have someone to drive it for him.

Purchasing a car then was much like purchasing a private jet today. The original marketing model, of course, was the horse-drawn carriage which, throughout the nineteenth century, had been owned by 'gentlemen' but driven by their lower class chauffeurs.

When Henry Ford introduced mass production of the automobile (see Figure 1.2) at his Highland Park plant in Michigan in 1913, he reduced the cost of the car dramatically and changed forever the type of person who owned one. The Model T Ford, which rolled off the Michigan assembly line at the rate of one every 24 seconds, went on sale for less than $400, one-tenth of the price of some of its rivals.

To help sales, Henry Ford increased his workers' wages to $5 a day, more than double the minimum wage at the time. At that rate it took a Ford worker a mere 80 days to earn enough to buy a Model T. By comparison, today it would take the best part of 113 days for a Ford production worker to earn enough to buy a basic Ford Taurus.

In 1908, which was its first year of production, Ford produced over 10,000 Model Ts, breaking all the industry's records. By the time the Model T went out of production in 1927 over 15 million of the cars had been sold in the USA. The automobile had rapidly become a product for the masses and an example to countless other companies of the benefits of scale. The idea of the moving assembly line, where the product came to the worker rather than the worker to the product, was rapidly adopted all over the world.

Figure 1.2 From the collections of Henry Ford Museum and Greenfield Village. Spooner and Wells, photographers: N.O. 1267

At first, mass markets were for the most part national markets. Ford, Chrysler and General Motors produced cars for Americans. Germans bought Volkswagen, the French bought Citröen and Peugeot while the British bought Morris and Vauxhall. Driving abroad invariably involved spotting a variety of car models that you had never seen before. Not then was there the universal and instantly recognisable 'global car'.

Globalisation

After the Second World War, however, companies were freed from the strictures of nationalist governments and could roam abroad in search of new markets and further economies of scale. The international financial markets that developed after the war enabled American companies in particular to raise finance abroad for foreign investment, and increasingly liberal foreign exchange rules on the remittance of dividends further persuaded firms to take the plunge. The book value of American companies' foreign direct investment rose from just over $7 billion in 1946 to over $70 billion in 1970 and well over $1 trillion in 1997.

European companies had for centuries invested in territories that fell within their empires (the British in India and South Africa, for example, the French in Indo-China), and they continued with a practice that they understood better than most. Contrary to the impression that most multinationals are American or Japanese, the combined investment in foreign companies of Britain, France, Germany and the Netherlands exceeds that of America and Japan put together.

The early post-war multinationals were organised in a

way that enabled them to maximise the gains to be made from economies of scale. They were not a diffuse group of relatively self-contained units that came together only in order to share a small group of common services or functions—brand names or corporate finance, for instance. They were firmly controlled in all things from the centre, and they closely followed corporate plans that were also drawn up at the centre.

Their activities were highly integrated with each other. In the early 1970s, for instance, IBM made components in several different countries, but these were all assembled into finished products within the United States. Hence any IBM computer to be found anywhere in the world was at that time an export from the United States. A number of American multinationals (Gillette, for example) still operate in much the same way today.

Financial bonus

Another consideration that drove the push for corporate gigantism in the twentieth century was the question of access to finance. Large companies had easier access to funds than did smaller companies and, by and large, they paid less for them.

In the UK this phenomenon was christened 'the Macmillan Gap' after the chairman of the government-appointed committee which identified and described it in a 1931 report on finance and industry. Companies that were too small to go public, but too large to continue to rely on the traditional source of funds to finance expansion—namely, the family—found it difficult to obtain long-term capital.

Despite setting up a special government body—the Industrial and Commercial Finance Corporation (the ICFC)—to fill this gap, the situation had not improved much by 1980 when the Wilson Committee (another group charged with looking into the UK's financial system) reported that:

> *"Compared to large firms, small firms are at a considerable disadvantage in financial markets".*

In the Anglo-Saxon world, part of the problem lay in the structure of the market for corporate finance. Loans for the small family firm traditionally came from local retail banks, while equity came from the family itself. Large companies, however, were able to turn to a group of specialist institutions, called merchant banks in the UK and investment banks in the United States. These specialists arranged packages of long-term finance—of debt, equity or whatever was required—and they also made big profits from arranging mergers and acquisitions.

At a time when capital was scarce, the specialists were able to charge high fees for being the portal through which any company needing a sizeable chunk of finance had to pass. And these high fees effectively acted as a barrier to small firms, preventing them from gaining access to the capital markets.

It was a version of Catch 22. In order to have access to the capital markets, companies needed to be a certain size. But in order to reach that size they needed access to the capital markets. It was also a recipe designed to make the big get bigger, and the small stay that way.

In continental Europe things were done differently.

There, and in Germany in particular, retail banks had a much greater control over the flow of corporate finance. The great success of the German Mittelstand, that country's vast resource of small and medium-sized companies, was often attributed to their easier access to the market for bank finance, a market where they competed on more equal terms with their nation's corporate giants.

This difference in forms of corporate finance has been used to explain the fact that there are fewer very large firms in continental Europe than there are in the UK (with the exception of some of the nationalised giants like Italy's IRI). But the difference has been disappearing in recent years as European economies have moved more towards the Anglo-Saxon model of equity funding and away from debt.

Nothing indicated this switch more powerfully than the decision by Daimler-Benz, the epitome of German manufacturing industry, 25% owned by the mighty Deutsche Bank, to have its shares listed on the New York Stock Exchange. Not only did that give it easier access to the massive pool of American capital, it also helped it subsequently to take over the Chrysler Corporation and to join a growing number of prominent American-German hybrids—for example, Bertelsmann and AOL; Deutsche Bank and Bankers Trust.

A death in the family

The need for outside finance to fuel the full possibilities of corporate growth has been the main force behind one of the great twentieth-century changes in the corporate landscape—the shift from the predominance of the family firm to the predominance of the public corporation. This was a switch from a corporate structure in which growth was only one of a mix of goals to a structure where growth, be it by organic means or by M&A, was by far the predominant goal.

At the beginning of the century the family-run firm was the norm in most industries, and not all family firms were small. When the Ford Motor Company totally dominated the automobile industry in the United States at the end of the First World War, the company was wholly owned by two men—Henry Ford and his son Edsel. Earlier, at the turn of the century, when the thread manufacturer J&P Coats had effectively controlled the world's textile industry, its board had been dominated by a handful of members of the Coats family.

Over the years, the number of large corporations that could be defined as family firms has dwindled in all major economies. In the UK most of that decline came in the second half of the century. In fact, the family firm survived the vicissitudes of the first 50 years (two world wars and a global depression) rather well. It has been estimated that at the end of the First World War 55% of the 200 largest companies in the UK had members of their founding families on the board. By 1930 that percentage had increased to 70%, and by the end of the Second World War it had fallen back, but only to 60%.

By the 1970s, however, the number of really large UK companies that could be called family firms had dwindled to a few—firms like the construction company McAlpine, the electronics group Ferranti and the Vesteys' food business. Although family connections remain in a few very large companies today—in retailers like Sainsburys and

Tesco in the UK, for instance, and in car companies like Ford and Fiat—none of these giants can be said any longer to be run like a family firm. As the economist Alfred Marshall put it, an essential ingredient of a family firm is that: 'The master's eye is everywhere'. Beyond a certain corporate size, that sort of control does not seem to work.

The transformation of the family firm in search of capital was in itself a promoter of growth. Many economists believe that family firms, when they reach a certain size, restrain growth. As very small businesses they are obviously ebullient promoters of it, but at a certain stage a sort of sclerosis sets in. Well-established family firms, for example, tend to resist mergers and acquisitions for fear of losing control to 'outsiders', and maybe (perish the thought!) of having the family's name disappear from over the front door of the company's headquarters.

Corporate longevity

Corporate survival is a powerful motivator for all companies. And since, on average, large companies live longer than small companies, firms have gone in search of size as a way of increasing their chances of survival.

The average large public company today can expect to live for 40–50 years, very much longer than the average family firm. Despite a widespread belief that the life cycle of the normal family firm is three generations ('One to build it, one to enjoy it, and one to destroy it') the truth is that few firms get beyond even the second generation. And those that do are often not in the hands of the founding families but of families that joined the business later as investors.

Unlike human beings, however, corporations seem to have no upper limit to their life span. The Swedish company Stora claims to have been mining copper seven centuries ago and only moved onto its current business, forest products, some time in the eighteenth century.

Japan's Mitsui can trace its history back to the seventeenth century, and for most of its life it has been run as a family business. A number of French family drinks firms can also trace their histories back for more than a couple of centuries. While in the UK there is a society called the Tercentenarians Club. To qualify, member firms must show that they have had a continuous history of at least 300 years.

Despite the fact that many of the very oldest companies in existence are still run as family firms, there is also a remarkable number of very large public corporations that have survived for the whole of the twentieth century and more. Coca-Cola, Kodak, Mercedes-Benz and Levis all feature in lists of the ten most powerful global brand names today. Yet all of them are more than 100 years old. The names Coca-Cola and Kodak were created within two years of each other in the late 1880s and share what savvy marketers now recognise to be two of the most powerful ingredients of a great brand—alliteration and the 'k' sound.

Another story of corporate endurance is even more remarkable. Mr Levi Strauss, a Bavarian immigrant to the United States, made the first pair of blue jeans with the distinctive metal rivets as long ago as 1850. The material he used was a special sort of cotton first manufactured in the French town of Nimes. Because it was from Nimes (*de Nimes*) it became known as denim. Mr Strauss's company is today a very large and well-known one, and his name is still synonymous with manufacturing excellence 150 years after he hammered his first rivets.

Throughout history, however, corporate size has provided no guarantee of durability. There have been countless examples of large companies unexpectedly (and swiftly) coming to an end. Of the 12 largest companies in the United States in 1900, only one (General Electric) survived until the end of the century—albeit in a very different shape. Of the two American airlines that dominated the skies until the 1970s, one (Pan Am) has disappeared altogether and the other (TWA) is a mere shadow of its former self.

The computer industry is particularly notable for giving birth to firms that have rapidly become giants and then shrunk into insignificance almost as quickly. Many of the leaders of the market for minicomputers in the early 1980s—firms like Nixdorf, Wang and Data General—completely failed to foresee the coming of the personal computer and the way in which it would undermine their very existence.

IBM, on the other hand, the leader in the computer industry's first era, the era of the mainframe, missed out on the minicomputer. But 'Big Blue' came bouncing back in the industry's third era, that of the PC.

Even the mighty IBM, though, needed a big slice of luck to get there. In 1980, when the company was one of the largest in the world, both in terms of turnover and market capitalisation, its planners predicted that the market for computers—there were probably no more than 70,000 on the whole of the planet at that time—would grow to all of 265,000 by the year 1990. In the event, there were more than 60 million computers in use by 1990.

The idea of corporate longevity as a motivator for growth fits in well with the model of the corporation developed by a former Royal Dutch/Shell corporate planner called Arie de Geus. In his book *The Living Company*, (Harvard Business School Press, US, 1997), Mr de Geus develops the idea that corporations are living organisms. As such their main purpose is survival.

De Geus's model has received much acclaim and provides a framework in which to think about corporate learning and about the adaptation of companies to their outside environment. It is a model that is particularly helpful for thinking about their survival in the twenty-first century.

How big can big be?

If you want to gasp about the size of the twentieth-century corporation then there is no better way than to draw comparisons with the gross domestic product of a nation. The biggest company in the world (by turnover) is General Motors and the value of its sales in 1998 was about the same as the GDP of countries like Austria and Denmark. Its turnover was twice the size of Egypt's GDP.

If that doesn't take your breath away then consider the fact that the price paid by BP in 1998 for fellow oil company Amoco ($61 billion) was enough to have bought the entire annual output that year of a country the size of Pakistan.

This sort of comparison did not just apply at the end of the century. In 1970, General Motors' turnover was still greater than the GDP of Austria and Denmark. The market capitalisation of Microsoft has just crossed over $500 billion. If that were the GDP of a country it would put

Microsoft in the top ten countries in the world (taking ninth place behind Spain).

The level of concentration of economic activity in the hands of these very large corporations has varied over time and according to country. In Europe, in the 1960s and 1970s, for instance, big business got relatively bigger—i.e. national production became more concentrated in the hands of the largest companies. In the 1980s, however, concentration declined, and by the end of the decade it was back more or less at the same level as in 1975.

Industrial concentration is a tricky thing to measure. By some measures the UK has more than its fair share of very large companies—giants like Royal Dutch/Shell, BP, BT and Glaxo Wellcome often feature among the world's top 25 (based upon market capitalisation). On the contrary, in Germany it is the notorious Mittelstand, small and medium-sized companies, that appear to dominate corporate life.

In 1970, however, the 100 largest manufacturing firms in what was then West Germany accounted for over 45% of their country's industrial production; the 100 largest manufacturing firms in the UK at the time accounted for only 40%. The level of concentration in UK manufacturing has declined since then, so the (perverse) difference between Big Company Britain and Small Firm Germany is probably even more pronounced today.

In the second half of the twentieth century, there was a dramatic change in the geographic distribution of the world's largest companies. In 1960 about 300 of the 500 largest corporations (as measured by *Fortune* magazine) were American; 150 of them were European and only 30 were Japanese. By 1990 that distribution had shifted so that the American tally was almost halved (down to 155) and the Japanese number increased to over 100. Europe's share increased slightly while the rest of the world's relatively small total more than doubled.

To a large extent this shift was the result of changes in exchange rates—the increase in the value of the Japanese yen over the period exaggerating the turnover of Japanese companies when converted for the purposes of comparison to a common currency (invariably the dollar). But it also highlighted the fact that Japan, the most successful economy in the world over the period, had built its success largely on the back of a number of giant interlocking corporations. This influenced the way in which a number of newly developing economies, such as South Korea, structured their industries.

Large companies had long been a feature of the Japanese industrial scene. The old-established *zaibatsu* that were compulsorily dismembered after Japan's defeat in the Second World War had dominated the economy for years— and to an extraordinary extent. At the beginning of the war, the ten biggest *zaibatsu* (which were then still controlled by a relatively small number of families) accounted for 35% of the total paid-up capital in Japan.

In South Korea, most of whose industrial growth has occurred over the last 30 years, large companies are even more dominant than they are in more mature economies. In 1990, one South Korean company alone (Samsung) accounted for one-fifth of the whole country's GDP.

Just as recently successful economies have been built on a small number of large firms, so have recently successful industries. 65% of the US market for PCs, for example, is in the hands of seven firms, and 72% of the mobile phones in use in the United States have been supplied by just three manufacturers (Motorola, Ericsson and Nokia). In most countries the supply of mobile-phone services is also concentrated in the hands of a couple of suppliers—in the UK, for instance, Vodafone and Cellnet have 77% of the market between them.

In some industrial sectors the dominance by a small number of large companies is the result of government intervention. In telecoms and airlines, for example, government ownership and control of 'national champions' in the days when industries were nationalised often ensured that the markets remained in the hands of a few, long after privatisation had ended. In 1998, for instance, 14 years after the privatisation of British Telecom, that firm still had 71% of the UK domestic market for fixed-line telephone traffic.

Governments have also helped to steer sensitive industries like defence and banking into the hands of only a few firms. It makes them feel they can more easily control them. In Europe, it is almost uncanny how many countries have a retail banking industry that is dominated by three or four firms. In the UK and France, for instance, 57% and 60%, respectively of total bank assets were in the hands of the top four banks in 1997. In smaller countries like Sweden and the Netherlands the level of concentration is such that the governments there would probably be obliged to block any proposal for further domestic mergers in the industry.

Services are special

The history of size in service industries has followed a slightly different course to that of manufacturing industry. Because there were fewer assembly-line processes where large economies of scale could be gained through mass production, service industries were slower to grow big and/or globalise. Retailing remained the preserve of local stores and corner shops until fairly recently. J. Sainsbury introduced the first self-service shop in 1950 and first hypermarket in 1977—at the dawn of the twenty-first century it had approximately 48 shops around London.

Financial services such as banking and insurance were being marketed only to the relatively privileged few until a couple of decades ago. For most of the twentieth century the mere possession of a bank account was the sign of a certain social status. Blue-collar workers were paid in cash and (usually) weekly. They bought things with cash and their savings were accumulations of cash placed in small local institutions. These local institutions joined together for the smooth processing of payments systems like cheques, but by and large they remained small.

In the United States in 1960 there were 13,216 banks. The largest bank then (Bank of America) had total assets that amounted to a mere 2.3% of America's GDP. By 1998 the largest American bank was Citigroup and its assets were equivalent to 8.9% of America's GDP.

The size of firms in service industries like retailing, and especially food retailing, grew when it was realised that there were economies of scale to be reaped in transport and logistics, and that these could be quite as effective as those to be gained from a manufacturing production line. This process was boosted by the widespread introduction of computers whose power enabled firms to track their stock and their transport continuously.

The computer also enabled financial services firms to enter and develop mass markets. A machine that was created for the rapid processing of complex data could not fail to have a major impact on an industry whose main business was the rapid processing of complex data—either of financial transactions (cheques, credit cards, etc) or of risks and rates of return on savings and loans.

As soon as the computer increased the capacity of financial institutions, firms went all out to sell their services to a mass market. In the UK, for example, in 1960, 29% of the population had a bank account; by 1997 that figure had risen to 77%.

The government's will

Big firms thrived throughout the twentieth century partly because economic growth and business processes worked in their favour. But they also thrived because the most powerful stakeholders in the corporation during that period had a vested interest in size. Governments, trade unions and management all found that large companies best suited their purposes.

The century began with a violent government reaction against the corporate gigantism of the nineteenth century. In 1890, the landmark Sherman Anti-Trust Act was passed in the United States. The biggest industrial giant in the world—the Standard Oil Company, put together by John D. Rockerfeller through a series of mergers with smaller prospectors and distributors—reorganised itself in order to avoid legal action.

But to no avail. The courts pursued it, and in 1911 a historic ruling by the US Supreme Court decreed that the company be broken up. The court said that 'the very genius for commercial development and organisation . . . soon begat an intent and purpose to exclude others'. Ever since the enforced dismemberment of the Standard Oil Company, however, large corporations have for the most part been left to themselves. A host of political, social and economic factors have worked almost continually in their favour.

The degree of industrial concentration that might have come about had that break-up not occurred can be gauged from the fact that 60 years later one part of that company (Standard Oil of New Jersey, now called Exxon) was still the third largest corporation in the world. At the same time, Standard Oil of California and Standard Oil of Indiana were the 11th and 15th largest corporations, respectively.

Managers, like owners, have a natural tendency to want to run something bigger than whatever it is that they are currently running. Promotion for a senior industry executive is generally marked by a move to a bigger job. Hence the most able managers migrate towards the larger companies, and they have a weather eye out for ways in which those companies can become even larger. A merger or acquisition, or a successful entry into a significant new market is the most enduring way for them to leave a mark.

Managers are also looking for greater size as a way to reduce competition. It is far easier for a small number of large firms to control prices and to establish a cartel than it is for a motley assortment of small ones.

Governments everywhere have introduced anti-trust legislation and other mechanisms in order to curb industry's excessive desire to stifle competition. But they have rarely been unequivocal in their opposition to Big Business.

Right-wing governments have tended to favour large corporations because they were frequently their major source of funding. And left-wing governments have liked large corporations because the trade unions (on whom they relied for funding and/or support) also preferred them. For powerful trade unions and their worker-members, large corporations gave surer guarantees of continuing jobs.

Government departments are themselves big (in fact in several countries like the UK and Sweden, the Civil Service arms of the government are the largest employers by far) and may tend to think that big is better. In any case, they have frequently been persuaded by businesses that becoming larger through merger is in the best interests of consumers (i.e. voters). The argument that a merger allowed the firm to reap economies of scale and to give benefits through lower prices for goods and services, more often than not won the day, especially if it was accompanied by firm denials of any job losses.

In 1989 a Harvard Business School professor, Rosabeth Moss Kanter, wrote a book (*When Giants Learn to Dance*, Simon & Schuster, US, 1990) advising big companies that it was time that they learnt how to be more nimble-footed. In effect, Ms Kanter said that they should learn how to behave like a large number of small firms. But, at the time, the momentum to get bigger was unstoppable, and the 1990s saw the biggest merger binge of all time.

The century, however, drew to a close in the shadow of a new high-profile anti-trust case, a case drawn up by the American government in response to the dominance of Microsoft in the market for PC operating systems.

The Microsoft case was one of a number of events in the later years of the century to suggest that the industrial and commercial environment was no longer working so strongly in favour of large corporations. In Chapter 2 we consider these events in greater detail.

2

The Threat to the Giants

IN THE LATTER YEARS OF THE TWENTIETH CENTURY, A number of powerful new forces came into play in the business world, and these forces began to undermine the existing industrial structure. As we saw in the last chapter, this structure had favoured giant corporations, in large part because of their ability to reap economies of scale and scope. The new forces presented the giants with an unprecedented challenge. If they were going to survive in the very different industrial landscape that was unfolding, they were going to have to radically rethink every aspect of their business.

Five of these new forces are proving to be particularly significant in this reshaping process, and they tend to work in favour of smaller firms and against the traditional giants. Taken individually, their threat does not seem insurmountable to the giants; taken together, however, their combined force is nothing short of breathtaking.

The five are:

1.   **The capacity of information technology (and especially of the Internet)** to enable new entrants to look for customers in many different industrial arenas. Not only have these firms proven themselves to be more agile and innovative than

the twentieth-century giants that they set out to topple, they are also in many cases built on a totally different economic model.

2.   **A shift in the balance of power between buyer and seller.** A variety of factors has helped to give the consumer more and more strength in the typical transaction between buyer and seller. It has taken a while for consumers to realise that big business no longer calls all the shots. As they become more aware of their power, they will begin to impose changes on the way that business is conducted. We have entered the age of the consumer as dictator, an age that is to have a revolutionary impact on markets and products.

3.   **Changing government attitudes towards the giants.** In most developed countries, governments have come to recognise that consumers (who are voters too) are becoming disenchanted with big business. This is leading these governments to give greater priority to the interests of consumers, by means of deregulation, for instance, and by taking a more consumer-centric view on issues such as the environment. Most significantly, however, government attitudes to competition policy, shaped by the mega-mergers that have become such a feature of many industrial sectors, have shifted sharply in favour of the consumer in recent years.

4.   **Industry convergence.** Recognising how crowded their own marketplace is, giant firms have developed a taste for new markets placing other giants under pressure, and making competition everywhere red-hot.

5. **A short-term focus** has come to predominate strategic thinking, especially in the United States where the financial markets' demands for short-term returns limit the ability of quoted companies to take the long-term view. As more and more economies adopt the US financial model, this effect has spread widely.

These five forces (see Figure 2.1) spell out nothing less than a new industrial order, a world in which the greatest corporations of the twentieth century are in danger of finding themselves extinct.

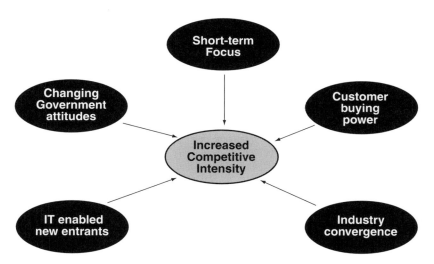

Figure 2.1   Competitive intensity is increasing due to the combination of five major forces

The capacity of IT

The most significant force pushing the twentieth-century giants off their pedestals is technology, and in particular, rapid developments in net-centric technology and the Internet. These are spawning a whole new generation of Internet-based firms, which play the business game by different commercial rules. These firms are both more agile and more innovative than the old giants. And they are predicated on an economic model in which economies of scale do not take centre stage.

The big advantage of being big used to be that it allowed a company to buy inputs more cheaply the more that it bought. And this gave it considerable competitive advantage in pricing its outputs. But the pursuit of economies of scale in this way is no longer the goal it once was. An increasing number of companies are coming to appreciate that the Internet can, in many cases, turn economies of scale upside down.

In their April 1999 report entitled 'Making Open Finance Pay', the Forrester Research Company gave examples of the way in which the Internet has completely undermined the pricing structure of a number of industries—particularly those with a high information content. In the era before the Internet (let's call it BI), it cost $100 to make an equity market order; afterwards it cost just $15, an 85% fall in price—far more than could have ever been gleaned from traditional economies of scale.

An annual subscription to the *Wall Street Journal*, BI, cost $329; via the Internet it costs a mere $49. And the cost of financial advice, BI, worked out at between 100 and 250 basis points; post-Internet, Forrester expects it to be around 50 basis points.

In addition, information technology is making the level at which diseconomies of scale kick in that much lower. Diseconomies of scale have always existed. The bigger a company becomes, the more complex is its structure and the more difficult it is to manage. In a world where flexibility and rapid change are essential characteristics of any successful organisation, any company (even a relatively small one) can find that its structure is too complex and rigid for it to keep up.

Professor Michael Porter of the Harvard Business School argues that 'new entrants, unencumbered by a long history in the industry, can often more easily perceive the potential for a new way of competing. Unlike incumbents, newcomers can be more flexible because they face no trade-offs with their existing activities.' As soon as a firm is so big that it has to make a trade-off (and it doesn't have to be very big to do that) it is liable to come up against the cost of complexity and to be vulnerable to newcomers that are not having the same experience.

Just as Microsoft seemingly appeared from nowhere to usurp the market of mighty IBM, so a few years later Netscape appeared overnight and threatened to undermine the market and the size of the by then mighty Microsoft. David beats Goliath. But then David grows big, and himself becomes as vulnerable as Goliath.

New age strategies

The typical corporate David of today pursues a strategy that focuses on building up turnover and a blue-chip list of clients by aggressive competitive pricing. Thanks to the new markets for corporate finance it is then able, at an early stage, to head for the stock market and an Initial Public Offering (IPO).

From the proceeds of the IPO, it proceeds to reward

handsomely the five or six key individuals on whom the firm's success depends. These key individuals are usually poached from elsewhere, either lured away from an old-established firm by their 'small is sexy' image, or else enticed from another recent start-up. (There is little loyalty in this new business world.) In the process, market incumbents are thrown dizzyingly off balance.

The strategy depends crucially on the way in which the stock market itself is changing. The growth of on-line trading has given these IT-based start-ups access to a new pool of IT-literate investors (the so-called day traders) who are prepared to take high risks when buying and selling from the comfort of their own PCs.

In the United States, the volume of online trading has been known to rise by as much as 50% in a couple of months. The US Securities and Exchange Commission reckoned recently that one in every four retail stock trades in the United States now takes place online. But its calculations are already out of date and are sure to be a serious underestimation.

Financial-service offerings of all sorts are sprouting over the Internet like mushrooms, and some of the early movers are reaping the richest harvest. At the US retail brokerage firm Charles Schwab, for instance, the firm's web site now accounts for more than half of all its securities trading. Three years ago the site did not exist.

But in eCommerce no one can rest on their laurels for long. Charles Schwab's main rivals are not, as they would have been a mere decade ago, Merrill Lynch or Dean Witter. Rather, they are unanticipated newcomers like E*Trade, Waterhouse Securities and Ameritrade, firms which have almost overnight become serious competitors in the long-established business of stockbroking, a business where not so long ago it could take several generations to build up significant market share.

The presence of online brokers in the stock market has helped similar firms in other industries to usurp the market position of the old timers.

Two academics, David Yoffie and Michael Cusumano, have called this new competitive game the 'judo strategy' (*Harvard Business Review*, January/February 1999), a competitive strategy in which (as in judo) small newcomers turn dominant players' strengths against them. The battle between Netscape and Microsoft they see as demonstrating many of the characteristics of judo strategy, the three main principles of which are rapid movement, flexibility and leverage.

In the early stages of the battle, Netscape moved very quickly, and it was the first company to offer a free stand-alone Internet browser. Later, however, it failed to be sufficiently flexible when in December 1995 Microsoft made its retaliatory move and announced that it would 'embrace and extend' its competitor's success.

At the time, Netscape turned down several opportunities to form partnerships with other companies, preferring to retain its independence. As a result it lost deal after deal when it tried to compete with Microsoft for distribution channels. The futility of its inflexibility was brought home when the company gave up its independence in November 1998 by accepting an offer worth $4.2 billion from AOL (America Online).

Messrs Yoffie and Cusumano argue that Netscape was rather more clever at using its leverage than it was at retaining its flexibility. By deciding to make its software compatible with existing non-proprietary UNIX systems, it left Microsoft stuck uncomfortably with its evangelical determination to convert the whole world to its own Windows operating software.

The opportunities for judo strategies in which nimble newcomers throw traditional old-timers off balance will proliferate as the Internet enables more and more firms to do business electronically. Electronic commerce, and in particular electronic commerce via the Internet, is having a more radical effect on corporate strategy and structure than anything since Henry Ford invented the assembly line in the last year before the First World War.

eCommerce

In many areas, such as banking, electronic technology is literally shrivelling the cost of goods and services. It has been estimated, for instance, that a banking transaction carried out via the telephone costs half as much as the same transaction conducted over the counter in a traditional branch; and that an ATM transaction costs a quarter as much.

But the category killer is the Internet: a banking transaction over the Internet costs a mere 1% of the cost of an over-the-counter transaction at a branch. This huge differentiator is summarised in Figure 2.2 and is enough to make the long-established 'bricks and mortar' establishments weep. Figures of that sort allow firms to establish substantial new businesses that can, very cheaply and rapidly, become competitive with the biggest and the best. This they do, not only by cutting prices and offering wider choices, but also (via electronic marketplaces like E-Loan and Annuity.net) by enabling consumers to make real-

Transaction method	Cost of transaction
Over the counter	$1.07
ATM machine	$0.27
Internet	$0.01

Figure 2.2   Costs of banking transactions via various mediums

time price comparisons, and (via electronic transfer systems like NextCard and OneSource) by allowing consumers to switch rapidly and frequently to the cheapest provider.

The potential of the Internet to undermine old business ways and institutions has only just begun to be felt. In 1996 23 million households around the world were estimated to have Internet access; three years later that number had risen to almost 70 million—and the great majority of those were in the United States.

Over the same period, the growth of business 'connectivity' was even more rapid. The number of businesses connected to the Internet in 1996 was around 40,000, a number that increased almost tenfold over the next three years.

Future growth is also sure to be phenomenal. A recent Andersen Consulting survey of businesses around Europe found that 82% of them expected that in five years' time they would be 'much more reliant' on eCommerce. In the UK and the USA, the figure was over 90%.

Commerce conducted via the Internet is already measured in tens of billions of dollars, and some analysts reckon it will be measured in hundreds of billions within a couple of years. Forrester Research reckons (modestly) that eCommerce will be worth $35 billion a year by 2002.

However big the market becomes, it is sure to shift the balance further in favour of small agile firms and against any organisation that is unable to take decisions quickly. In the process, however, it is also undermining traditional concepts of corporate size. A whole new generation of Internet-based companies are being valued on the stockmarket at sums which, whatever they are (and in many cases they defy conventional yardsticks), can certainly not be described as small.

The *Financial Times* of 9 February 1999 set them in context:

> *The market capitalisation of Yahoo!, the leading Internet company, has appreciated by 3,800% since 1996 and is now 480 times expected earnings for 1999. Yahoo! is worth more than Texaco or Merrill Lynch. America Online, the largest Internet company, has risen by 34,000% since 1992 and is now worth 273 times expected earnings for the year to June. That makes it bigger than Ford or Disney. Both companies would be in the Japanese top 10, and AOL would be in Europe's top 10, ahead of Nestlé, Shell or UBS.*

America Online bigger than Shell? And Yahoo! now advertising that it is bigger than British Airways? It's staggering. But it's not unprecedented. The same *FT* article points out that Microsoft's average annual compound growth in earnings was over 40% between 1985 and 1995. During that time its share price rose by 3,500%. The dramatic increase in Internet stocks can be seen in Figure 2.3.

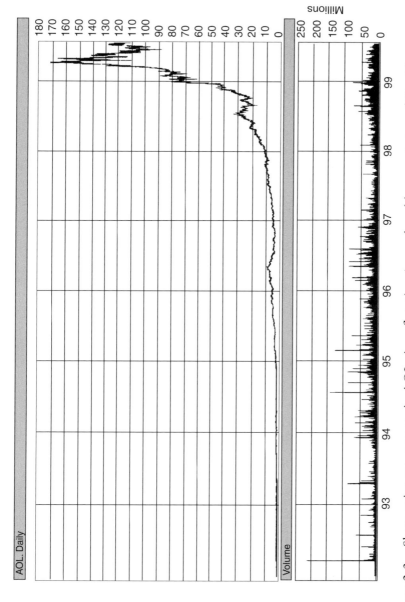

Figure 2.3   Share price movements in AOL since flotation (reproduced by permission of Big Charts at www.BigCharts.com)

The eCommerce hopefuls remain small, however, in at least two important respects. In the first instance, however big they are, and by whatever yardstick, they know that they have to continue to behave as if they are small. Only that way can they remain as agile and competitive as the day they were first launched onto the market.

Secondly, their profits are almost invariably small. Indeed, hardly any of them have yet made a profit. Even the most famous, the bookseller Amazon, cheers when its losses get smaller. Yet at the end of the millennium Internet-based companies had stratospheric stock market valuations. America Online, for example, was valued at $123 billion, up a staggering 57,662% on its initial IPO price. In fact, there were 66 companies that were up over 1,000% on their issue prices.

Some analysts say they cannot see how these firms are ever going to make big profits. For it is fundamental to eCommerce that the customer is in control, and he or she can search the Web rapidly, ruthlessly seeking out the cheapest price. eCommerce, these analysts claim, is a business of, at best, low margins and, at worst, no margins.

From there they go on to predict doom and gloom for the Internet upstarts as they break every rule in the book of corporate valuation. Technical glitches—such as the ones which brought down the systems of eBay, the most successful online auctioneer, in May and June 1999 (and knocked a fifth off its share price, the equivalent of almost $4 billion)—only serve to confirm their scepticism.

But conventional measures and expectations are inappropriate for the revolution that these firms represent. Many could not see a way in which Henry Ford was going to sell all the cars that were about to tumble off his assembly lines in 1913. But a brilliant piece of lateral thinking (doubling the wages of Ford's workers) soon created a ready market for them.

Cherry picking

A big part of the threat of the newcomers comes from the fact that in many cases they are able to 'cherry pick' their customers. Consider the following: in the average UK supermarket, 10% of the customers account for 50% of the profits. At an average bank in the UK, 40% of the customers produce 100% of the profits. One UK bank is in the dangerous position of having 100% of its profits come from just 20% of its customers.

This is these companies' Achilles heel. For if a cherry picker were able to identify the 10% of a supermarket's customers who provide it with 50% of its profit, and then make that 10% an irresistible proposal, imagine the damage that would cause to the supermarket in question.

But whatever that damage, it would be nothing compared with the instant obliteration in store for the bank which gets 100% of its profits from 20% of its customers, if and when an Internet upstart is able to identify that 20% and make them an offer that they cannot refuse. Such a day is not far off. It is certainly much nearer than most banks dare to imagine.

Viewed from the other side, the big question becomes, why are banks and supermarkets carrying on with all that unprofitable business? After all, in most cases they are not being compelled to provide a public service for which there are other goals than profit.

Shift in the balance of power

The second major force reshaping the industrial landscape is the extraordinarily rapid shift in power taking place between sellers and buyers. This has been influenced by a number of factors, the most obvious of which has been the sharp and unprecedented increase in consumer spending over the past few decades. Average incomes in the United States increased by 24% in real terms in the last 30 years of the twentieth century. In Japan, the increase was an even more dramatic 60%.

The more money that people have, the more they are able to exercise choice in making their purchases. And a consumer with choice is a consumer with power.

At the same time as consumers were becoming a lot wealthier, many of the products and services that they wanted to buy were becoming a lot cheaper. This was not just the things that everybody was aware of, things like computer hardware where Moore's Law encapsulated the fact that the price of semiconductors (and the price of the products into which they were embedded) fell even as their power increased. It also included a host of less obvious things—like a bar of chocolate, for instance, a bottle of wine or a litre of petrol. All of these were significantly less expensive in real terms in 1999 than they had been a quarter of a century earlier.

The taming of inflation over the same period added to this effect. In the latter years of the century, consumers in the world's largest economies—the United States, the EU and Japan—began to grow accustomed to living with historically low rates of inflation. Consumer price rises in these countries, which in the 1970s had frequently been in double figures, and in the 1980s were usually somewhere between 5% and 10%, rarely in the 1990s rose above 5%.

The tight monetary policies that brought this about led consumers to believe that not only had governments got the know-how to stifle inflation, they also had the political will.

In the past, high inflation (and the expectation of more) had injected a sense of urgency into consumers' purchasing decisions. If they did not buy goods and services immediately, they were sure to have to pay more for the same things (in nominal if not in real terms) a few months down the line. Sellers could relax in the knowledge that restless consumers were being driven into their arms.

Nowadays, by contrast, consumers are increasingly the ones who relax, confident in the knowledge that if they do not buy something today they will be able to get it at much the same price in the not-too-distant future. At the moment, $1,000 buys you more and more computing power the longer you wait. Some firms are now giving PCs away for free.

Even when prices don't fall, quality rises. The price of cars may not have changed much in recent years, either in real terms or as a percentage of the average wage, but the quality and durability of the average car has improved dramatically. That makes it significantly cheaper—because it consumes less fuel, needs less frequent servicing, and lasts longer in reasonably good condition.

For the giants of the twentieth century, brought up on a world of inflationary expectations, this has been a rude shock. Much of their forward planning was based on an almost unquestioned assumption that prices would rise indefinitely. As Jack Welch, the chairman of General Electric, wrote in his company's annual report for 1998: 'Inflation has yielded to deflation as the shaping economic force'. This has compelled companies to think again about their basic cost structure.

For example, one of the costs that companies have blithely assumed will rise indefinitely has been the cost of labour. In a non-inflationary economy it is a heavy burden to carry a labour force that either has expectations of a perpetual annual pay rise or has a contractual right to one.

The shift in favour of consumers and away from buyers is not about to end or to be reversed. Developments in Internet technology are just beginning to put almost incredible new power into the hands of consumers. Sophisticated search engines already allow them to trawl the Net and to find the best deals on offer with no more effort than a few keystrokes.

In time, the technology will develop further and allow producers to 'push' products towards consumers. Instead of relying on consumers to go out and look for them, producers will turn the tables and set out to search electronically for consumers. Ever more sophisticated databases will enable them to pinpoint those consumers who will be most interested in the offerings that they are making at that moment. Consumers will merely have to lie back and be served.

At the same time, firms like priceline.com are forcing down the price of goods and services by bringing the ancient art of the auction house to bear on a whole range of new areas. And these new electronic auction houses need be no further away than the room where you keep your PC.

Buying loyalty

What on earth is going to persuade empowered buyers to repeatedly seek value from one provider rather than from another? Many of them are still reeling from the job cuts of the early 1990s. They are nowhere near as confident about economic prospects for the future as they were in the 1980s. As the Asian economic crisis in the early and middle part of 1998 demonstrated, an economic blip in any part of the world can today ripple rapidly across the globe and undermine confidence.

Consumers are also far cleverer than they used to be. This is not just to say that many more of them have had a tertiary education than in any generation previously, though that is undoubtedly a key feature of the consumer of today. It is also a comment about the fact that consumers now are much more savvy about the way that manufacturing and retailing works. They know about retailers' margins, and they are prepared to shop around for a better price and a better deal in a way that their mothers and fathers never did.

We hear a lot about the 'death of loyalty', and rightly so. Customer loyalty is, however, not yet entirely dead. Keeping it alive is one of the biggest business challenges for firms today.

The idea of loyalty received a great deal of attention in the 1990s, particularly in the work of Fred Reichheld following an article in the *Harvard Business Review* in March 1993 in which he argued that loyalty was closely related to profitability.

Reichheld claimed that when a company consistently delivered superior value and won customer loyalty, its market share and revenues went up and the cost of acquiring new customers went down. The company was then able to pay its workers better; overall job satisfaction increased; customers were served better, and they became more inclined to stay loyal to the company.

It is often surprising to work out just how much a loyal

customer can be worth. Suppose a family of four buys their groceries from the same supermarket for ten years. Their weekly bill might easily average over £80—which means that their total spending at that one shop in ten years is in excess of £40,000.

In ten years a family is very unlikely to spend that much money on cars. Yet think of the attention that car dealers lavish on their individual customers. And then think of the attention (or, rather, the lack of it) that supermarkets give to their regular shoppers.

It is now widely appreciated how much cheaper it is to retain the loyalty of an old customer than it is to win the business of a new one. But that does not mean to say that it is entirely without cost. Customers have to be persuaded to remain loyal. Branding is the traditional way of building loyalty to products and services. But firms have to look beyond that to determine what it is that establishes loyalty to the providers of solutions. A number have begun to experiment with things like 'loyalty cards' and air miles. But that is only the beginning.

Global and local

Another area where the new-found power of consumers is in evidence is in their growing hostility to the uniformity of much of the world's manufactured products. There is a new demand for customised tailored solutions that affirm the uniqueness of the individual who buys them. This demand is being fuelled by the way in which technology is beginning to enable firms to 'mass customise' goods and services, to use some of the techniques of mass production to do just the opposite.

This change is having a significant impact on the way

in which traditional multinationals behave. Many global corporations are beginning to realise that the tastes of local consumers are powerfully different and to be ignored at their peril. Rather than riding roughshod around the world's markets, pushing the same products into all of them regardless, they are beginning to take account of the local tastes of different customers in different regions.

In 'The End of Corporate Imperialism', an award-winning article by C. K. Prahalad and Kenneth Lieberthal that appeared in the July–August 1998 issue of the *Harvard Business Review*, the authors argued that in the future multinationals will be as much affected by the big new markets that they enter (China, India, Indonesia and Brazil, for instance) as those markets will be affected by them. This, they point out, is in sharp contrast to the past, the age of corporate imperialism, a time when the big American multinationals in particular were invariably very American in their culture, their employees and their management style. In addition, a large percentage of the inputs to their final products were imported from the United States.

This shift, the authors say, will force these giant multinationals to rethink 'every element of their business models in order to be successful'. A growing number of multinational companies will be forced to think of themselves as 'multi-domestic', as a loosely associated network of smaller organisations where the range of central control is clearly defined and limited.

Changing government attitudes

Governments can smell the way a wind is blowing, and in many countries they have acknowledged the shift in the balance of power from producers to consumers. In some cases, through deregulation for instance, they have actually contributed to it. The deregulation of the European telecommunications industry, for instance, has led to falls of as much as 89% in the price of international calls over the past ten years. And the state-led break-up of distributors' oligopolies (for instance in the UK car industry) is likely to push this effect even further.

But, more significantly, governments have increasingly come to align themselves with consumers' interests. For it has been brought home to them more and more forcefully that consumers are voters too. A government that does not bring home the economic bacon to its electorate is going to have a hard time getting re-elected.

One of the things to which consumers have been demonstrating an increasing aversion in recent years is big business. In a regular MORI poll in the UK, for instance, people are asked whether they agree that the profits of large British companies help make things better for everyone who buys their goods and services. In 1970, when the poll was first held, 53% agreed with the proposition. By 1980 that figure had risen slightly to 56%. But since then it has fallen remorselessly. In the poll held in early 1999 only 25% agreed with the proposition. As many disagreed with it in 1999 as had agreed with it in 1970. This slump in consumer confidence of large British companies is illustrated in Figure 2.4.

The mood of many governments in recent years has followed this shift in consumers' attitudes towards 'Big Business'. The centre-left parties that now rule in the United States and most of western Europe are neither in the thrall of trade unions, nor of businessmen and managers.

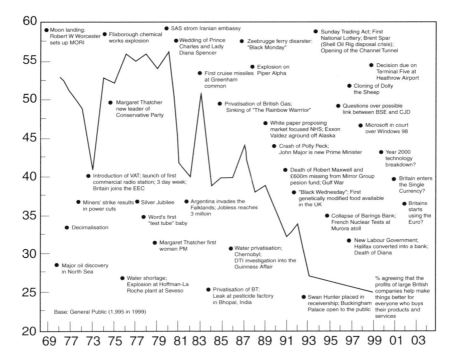

Figure 2.4   Percentage of population agreeing that large British companies help make things better for those who buy their products and services

They are listening more and more to consumers as they become increasingly vocal in their objections to the power of big business. This stretches from the environmentalists' complaints about big oil firms and mining companies, to consumers' distress at what they see as the cavalier attitudes to health demonstrated by big tobacco firms in their marketing of cigarettes and, more recently, by big food companies in their production of genetically modified crops.

The way that the British government had to back down on its initially favourable stance on genetically modified crops was a telling demonstration of the rising power of the consumer.

The switch of government attitudes in line with the interests of consumers is demonstrated more generally by the declining significance of 'consumer movements'. These were most prominent in the United States in the 1960s and 1970s under the guidance of Ralph Nader, but they mushroomed everywhere in the 1970s and 1980s as consumers became more and more aware of their own power.

Today, however, on many of the movements' favourite battlegrounds—consumer safety and the provision of information, for example—they find themselves on the same side as their governments. For most of them, this is a relatively novel experience.

Anti-monopoly

Perhaps the most significant way in which governments have aligned themselves with consumers' interests in recent years has been in their attitude to industrial concentration, brought about in large part by mergers and acquisitions (M&A). The rash of mega-mergers that were such a feature of the industrial scene in the second half of the 1990s caused several industries and markets to push up against the limits of acceptable levels of concentration. The authorities in Canada, for example, have made it clear that it is most unlikely that they will allow any more mergers among that country's major domestic banks.

In both Europe and North America, the anti-trust authorities have been active like never before. One of the best known (and busiest) of the EU's commissioners is the man in charge of competition. Among other things, he has turned his attention in recent years to Europe's airline industry, its oil industry and its chemicals industry, all areas where he has expressed concern that levels of concentration are not acting in the consumers' best interests.

In 1998, for example, the EU showed how determined it was to break the stranglehold that the big airlines had on the all-important landing slots at key airports—and the ability that this gives them to throttle small airlines in their infancy. Karel Van Miert, the EU commissioner in charge of competition at the time, decided not only that American Airlines and British Airways should hand over 267 slots at Heathrow and at Gatwick, London's major airports, as part of the strategic alliance between the two companies, but also that they should receive no compensation for doing so. In line with Britain's deputy Prime Minister John Prescott, he maintained that the slots were not the property of the airlines but rather of the community—i.e. of taxpayers, voters and consumers.

The biggest stand-off between government and big business, however, came with the anti-trust complaint brought in 1998 by America's Justice Department against Microsoft. For many years Microsoft's dominance of the market for PC operating software had raised questions about its ability to manipulate prices in its own favour and against the interests of consumers.

The case was described by *The Economist* as 'the most important competition case of the decade', and probably the most important since 'Ma Bell' was ordered to be dismantled in the early 1980s.

The Microsoft case was followed shortly afterwards by the filing of anti-trust charges against Intel, the world's largest manufacturer of semiconductors. The two companies stand at the centre of the fastest-growing industry in the world. By the charges levelled against them, however, the US government sent clear signals to say that no industry, however dynamic and important for economic growth, was immune from the legislation's basic concern for consumer protection. That was not a message that they had attempted to convey in the previous decades.

The Economist argued that these cases were important partly because they demonstrated 'the new ways that economists have found to think about competitive behaviour'. And, in particular, about the predatory way in which big companies crush little ones.

'For most of this century,' it claimed, 'the branch of economics that studies competition has been an intellectual backwater. But now, as trustbusters weigh an unprecedented number of mergers and all sorts of novel business arrangements that would reshape industries from publishing to defence . . . the intellectual tide has turned. The economic ideas of the 1970s and 1980s argued overwhelmingly that government activism in competition was often unwarranted and counterproductive. Now they are giving way to new thinking that justifies tougher anti-trust enforcement.'

The new thinking was partly spurred by dissatisfaction with traditional ways of measuring competitiveness. A key measure is the Herfindahl–Hirschman Index which adds up the squares of the market shares of all the firms competing in a market. A high figure indicates a high degree of concentration and conditions in which prices can be maintained above their natural free-market level—i.e. in favour of producers and against consumers.

This measure has always had trouble with markets like that for soft drinks in America. There, Pepsi-Cola and Coca-Cola's duopoly gives a very high Herfindahl–Hirschman index. Yet price competition between the two cola giants is notoriously fierce. Other powerful duopolies where fierce price competition undermines the index's value are in the commercial aircraft industry (between Airbus and Boeing) and in the market for washing powders (between Unilever and Procter & Gamble).

In what *The Economist* described as: 'One of the most startling developments in industrial organisation, economists have now concluded that 'the market' does not necessarily matter'. They are now attempting more narrowly to judge whether an arrangement such as a merger would drive prices higher than they would otherwise have been.

Corporate marketing departments are moving to a similar position, albeit from a different direction. They are placing less emphasis on defining the classic 'market' and their share of it, and placing more emphasis on vaguer concepts like 'market space'.

This new thinking has brought about some unexpected decisions. In the proposed merger between two office-equipment suppliers in the United States—Staples and Office Depot—for example, there was no problem with the traditional measures of market share. There are lots of suppliers of office equipment in the United States.

But when the trustbusters looked into the prices at which each firm sold each of its products, its computers threw up a pattern. Staple's prices were lower in cities where Office Depot also had an outlet than they were in cities where it did not. A court blocked the merger on the grounds that this was evidence that Staples would raise its prices to consumers in these cities after a merger.

The Economist concluded: 'The [new economic] theories will, without doubt, motivate enforcers to investigate business behaviour that hitherto would have raised no eyebrows. They will come to understand new ways in which businesses acquire excessive market power. Consumers should be grateful.'

Keeping consumers grateful will be increasingly important for governments in the twenty-first century. For the giants of the twentieth century, it will be absolutely vital.

Industry convergence

The fourth main force shifting industrial structures is the widespread intrusion of all players into the markets of others. More and more companies are entering new and, for them, non-traditional markets.

The entry of supermarkets into financial services is one of the most obvious examples. Bankers who thought that they knew their competition like the back of their hand, which was hardly surprising since in many markets that competition had scarcely changed for decades, have suddenly found that they have to contend with rivals like Tesco in the UK and Carrefour in France.

At the same time they are having to cope with the challenge from even less conventional rivals—firms like Virgin Direct, a virtual organisation that launched a banking service without any brick and mortar distribution channel. Billions of pounds of assets have left the banks' balance sheets and fled to the books of these non-banking institutions. It will be no easy task to get them back.

The banks are responding to the challenge by branching out themselves. For instance, 68% of the bankers interviewed in a joint survey carried out by Andersen Consulting and the UK's Chartered Institute of Bankers, said that they believe their institution will be supplying non-financial products in the future. With newcomers cherry-picking their customers, banks have little choice but to look for pastures new. Their only alternative is to watch while their market share and their margins are remorselessly eroded.

A number of financial institutions have already started to move into new businesses. The UK's Direct Line insurance company, for example, offers its customers a breakdown service—not for emotional breakdowns when customers need to make a claim (though such a service might be on offer in the future!) but for car breakdowns.

Through its links with over 150 independent car dealers, Direct Line arranges for customers' cars to be collected from their homes in the morning, repaired during the day, and delivered to their owners' place of work before 5.30 p.m. the same evening.

Industrial convergence is happening right across the board. The Italian computer company Olivetti, for example, has taken the plunge into the telecoms business. (Olivetti's $65 billion take-over of Telecom Italia, a company six times its size, was at the time the biggest deal that Europe had ever seen.) Olivetti, originally one of the world's best-known typewriter brands, first reinvented itself as a personal-computer company, and then when that business ran out of steam it trampled into telecoms—in about as big a way as possible.

Utilities are another area where there are poachers afoot. Power generators are going into electricity distribution and water companies seem to be flowing everywhere. Much of this is being assisted by government deregulation of these industries. The UK has been gradually opening up its electricity market, for instance, and finally threw the doors of the retail market open to full competition in May 1999.

Perhaps the greatest convergence among utilities is occurring in the gas and electricity sectors. These two industries are increasingly becoming one. Andersen Consulting reckons that within ten years 40% of Europe's electricity will be produced from gas—at the moment the figure is under 15%. In the United States, almost 75% of all electricity is already generated from gas. Fourteen of the 30 largest gas and electricity firms in America made convergence-related acquisitions or mergers in the two years from 1996 to 1998.

But that does not mean that the gas and electric utilities are sewing up the two businesses for themselves. Some of the major oil companies are trying to get into both. Texaco, for example, earns almost $3 billion a year from its electricity and gas trading businesses. A senior vice president of the company has been quoted as saying that Texaco intends to be 'a global energy firm, not just an integrated oil company.' There is plenty of speculation too that BP and/or Royal Dutch will make a big move into the power generation business.

Big cash-rich oil companies like these are being compelled to look to new businesses because of the depressed state of their own. Persistent low oil prices have been eating away at the margins of the oil majors for a number of years now. If they want to stay as big as they once were, they will have to find something new to do.

The reasons

There are two main reasons for much of the recent industry convergence:

1. In the first place, companies are deciding that their own **markets are getting too crowded** and that they need to move into new ones in order to find a bit of space. This is particularly obvious in an industry like banking. In a number of countries in Europe, the degree of concentration in the industry is such that there are few take-over options left that will not incur the displeasure of the anti-trust authorities. So firms either have to go abroad, which is never easy, or they have to go into something new.

2. Secondly, firms are moving into new fields in order to be able to offer a **broader range of products and services** to their existing customers—those customers having indicated forcefully that they will take their business elsewhere (all of it, that is) if their demands are not met. This is true in utilities, for example, where big customers in the United States are increasingly turning to companies like Enron to supply them with all their energy needs. Given the choice, they prefer to work with a single supplier.

Convergence has been helped by the fact that many firms have spent a good number of years identifying and homing in on their core competencies. It has been fashionable for them to examine carefully what they are good at, and do more of it, and to get rid of what they are not so good at, and do less of it.

This has involved them in shedding a number of peripheral activities. But it has also involved them in realising that the things that they do well are not necessarily confined to the industry into which they as a firm have traditionally been categorised. At BP's Wytch Farm oil refinery in the south of England, for instance, the oil major considers itself to be in the business of environmental management. The drilling and many of the other oil-related operations and processes there have been outsourced to others—often smaller specialist firms.

The idea that one of BP's core competencies is environmental management has taken the company into the area of solar energy. BP is now one of the UK's biggest manufacturers of solar panels. A few years back, other manufacturers of solar panels would not have seen the huge oil firm as a potential rival.

But in all industries, new rivals are appearing from the most unlikely directions. Sandra Vandermerwe, a professor of management at London's Imperial College, quotes the example of a busy American IT manager who bought 20 Apple Mac PCs for her company. The computers were ideal for her purposes, but she made the mistake of purchasing them from her local 'value-added retailer'. The retailer was at the time giving a 20% discount to the list price.

When the machines were delivered, they were dumped in their boxes in the firm's reception area. The manager had to call in extra people to help move them into the offices, and it took her and an assistant two weeks to get rid of the old machines, replace them with the new ones, and show the staff how the two differed.

The manager told her sorry story to as many people as she could persuade to listen. One of them happened to be a representative of a courier company, and he invited her to let his company know when she was next looking to buy computers and to invite it to bid for the contract. The courier company was not only able to buy computers for clients; it was also able to deliver them and install them.

Old dogs

A host of firms are becoming poachers because they are seizing the opportunities that electronic commerce provides for them to do new things in different ways. It is not just upstarts backed by a surfeit of Californian capital which find the prospect of Internet-based new business pleasing. A sample of senior executives in Europe and the United States told Andersen Consulting in a recent survey that they thought that banking was the sector most likely to 'lead the field in the development of eCommerce'.

Other well-established firms are going to make sure that the Internet upstarts, the so-called 'dot com' stocks don't have the new electronic business arena all to themselves. At the end of 1998, for instance, the Japanese consumer electronics giant Sony declared that it was going to start selling financial services at rock-bottom prices via the Internet. Such services will include securities trading and both life and non-life insurance.

The Internet upstarts themselves do not stay in one industrial category for long either. They are constantly and restlessly looking for new opportunities. The well-known online auction house priceline.com, for example, best known for its auctions of airline tickets and hotel rooms, has now applied its talents to mortgages.

Some of the old-style firms with established reputations in other areas are proving no slouches at Internet-based business either. In the UK, the market's leading electrical retailer Dixons shot from nowhere to become Britain's biggest Internet service provider (ISP), gaining one million subscribers in the space of five months at the end of 1998.

Its Freeserve service revolutionised the ISP market in the UK by taking its revenues from advertisers and electronic service providers rather than from subscribers—to whom the service was offered free. Despite being as yet non-profit-making, the service had the effect of boosting Dixons' share price sharply. Freeserve was floated on 26 July 1999 with a market capitalisation value of £1.5 billion. At the end of the first day's trading shares closed up 60 pence at 210 pence per share. Not surprisingly, other firms from all sorts of industries are now looking to follow Dixons' example.

Short-term focus

The final force remoulding today's industrial landscape, and upending the traditional assumption that large firms are at an advantage vis-à-vis their smaller rivals, is the growing demand for short-term performance.

This is not an entirely new phenomenon. Large American quoted companies have been accustomed for years to the time-consuming scrutiny of Wall Street analysts, and the demands from brokers for constant improvement. And in the UK in the 1980s, Asil Nadir, the founder of wonder-stock Polly Peck, was notorious for spending days with his eyes glued to a Reuters monitor on which was exhibited the fluctuating price of Polly Peck's shares. Early to appreciate that from his company's share price all good things flowed (including his own wealth), Mr Nadir was being investigated for fraudulently manipulating that share price when he fled the UK in May 1993.

The pressure for short-term performance, however, has increased both in depth and breadth. There is no corner of the quoted world—be it New York or the remotest emerging market—where analysts do not pop up demanding time, attention and results.

These analysts get seriously upset these days if companies do not at least meet their forecast earnings every single quarter. And an upset analyst is not a pretty sight. A company's status can be changed from 'recommended buy' to 'sell' in as much time as it takes to make four keystrokes and send them down the line.

That has a host of implications that can turn any CEO's happy morning into a nightmare of an afternoon. First, it can well put his job on the line. Eckhard Pfeifer, a former chief executive of Compaq, was not the first nor the last head of a leading company to have been given his cards for little more than the market's displeasure at one quarter's bad results.

Secondly, an analyst's thumbs down will depress any company's share price, and that will make it more expensive for the company to borrow money or to raise new equity in future. It will also make it more difficult for the company to attract the small pool of talented individuals on which companies are increasingly coming to rely.

The way that companies entice these individuals is more and more based on giving them share options. If the value of the company's share price (and therefore of its share options) falls, these individuals will themselves easily fall into the arms of the nearest head-hunter.

Of course, the new Internet start-ups are also under pressure to perform in the short term. They are under the financial market's beady eye almost before they have hatched from their chrysalis. But they do have an advantage over their older and larger rivals. For, should they get things wrong, they can more quickly redirect their efforts than can, say, a Compaq or a BP.

Moreover, the market puts far less emphasis on their profits or, more likely, their losses than it does those of a well-established firm. This is because the market value of the dot-com stocks lies so much in their future promise, and not in their past performance. And future promise is intangible and immeasurable.

Immediate results from the lab

The growing need to focus on the very short term is also having a radical effect on corporate research and development. Gone are the days when R&D was focused on 'discovery', when boffins gathered in research laboratories and spent lots of time and R&D dollars 'trying things out'.

In some industries, old-style research is still essential for progress and for growth. Pharmaceuticals companies' R&D departments search expensively for the next blockbuster drug, the next Zantac or Prozac or AZT. But it is a far more hasty and systematic process than it used to be.

In today's world, research energies are focused far less on the glamorous 'eureka' type of invention, the sudden blinding flash of light that changes the world—and an industry or two along with it—the invention of the telephone, for instance, or the electric light bulb. For the life of invention today is brief. If a company cannot get the fruits of its research to market in double quick time, the whole effort is likely to have been wasted. There is always an alternative or imitator waiting impatiently in the wings.

So companies today are more concerned with the type of invention that shows up in incremental improvements in processes. Firms have found that not only is this far less capital intensive, but also that its results are far more immediate in their impact on the bottom line.

Much of this type of effort is focused on finding new ways of using information technology to improve business performance. And this is an area in which large old-established giants may well be at a disadvantage.

In *The Innovator's Dilemma: When new technologies cause great firms to fail*, (Harvard Business School Press 1997), an influential book written by a Harvard academic, the author Clayton Christensen points to the great difficulty that large organisations often have in keeping abreast of new technologies, in particular what he calls 'disruptive technologies'. These include technologies like the Internet that radically change the business environment and typically enable new markets to emerge. 'When faced with a threatening disruptive technology', he wrote, 'people and processes in a mainstream organisation cannot be expected to allocate freely the critical financial and human resources needed to carve out a strong position in the small emerging market.'

This leaves such markets open to small newcomers. He also notes:

> *Those large established firms that have successfully seized strong positions in the new markets enabled by disruptive technologies have done so by giving responsibility to commercialise the disruptive technology to an organisation whose size matched the size of the targeted market. Small organisations can most easily respond to the opportunities for growth in a small market. The evidence is strong that formal and informal resource allocation processes make it very difficult for large organisations to focus adequate energy and talent on small markets, even when logic says they might be big someday.*

One of the main ways of being innovative in this brave new business world is reserved it seems for the small. Giants beware.

The tornado effect

Each of the five forces that we have considered in this chapter is having a powerful effect on business strategy and structure in its own right. But together they are producing a whirlwind that is making them far more powerful than the sum of their parts. Together they are bringing about the greatest level of competitive intensity ever seen in the industrial world.

The giants of the twentieth century spent much of their time suppressing competition—either through private agreements among themselves or by persuading governments that restricting competition was good for a nation's general economic health. And they became very good at it.

But that skill is not going to be of much use to them in the twenty-first century. For the power of unfettered competition is being unleashed upon the business world. And it is not like anything that the giants have experienced before. They are, almost literally, being left gasping for air as the competitive whirlwind sweeps past them and saps away their energies.

To survive, they need to consider carefully the various effects that these forces are having (and are going to have) on their business. For example:

1. **Products will tend to be turned into commodities.** This requires firms to become either a low-cost producer or to organise their business in such a way that cost comparisons are no longer possible.

2. **Consolidation and convergence will continue across the industrial spectrum.** In this case, companies need to be constantly putting a toe into new waters, to be acquiring smaller players in specialist niche areas or in new geographical regions.

3. **There will be a growing awareness that no company can be good at everything,** and that competition will be too fierce and glaring for them to hide whatever it is that they are bad at. This makes core competencies the key thing to focus on, for therein lies the company's value-adding franchise.

4. **New challengers will continue to appear thick and fast.** To have any hope of fending them off, companies will have to cut their 'time to market' down to the bone.

5. **Customers will become less and less loyal.** Companies that want to foster something resembling loyalty in their customers will have to look way beyond the simple provision of products and services.

Each firm needs to think through the impact of the five forces on its own business individually, for they will be affecting and changing each business differently. But there is a number of broad changes that apply across the board and that will be required of all companies which intend to take on the challenges of the twenty-first century. These changes involve a fundamental reconfiguration of the corporation around three dimensions:

1. The nature of what they offer to their customers.
2. The nature of the relationship they have with their customers.
3. Their level of virtualisation—i.e. the extent to which a firm tries to do everything itself, or works with third parties to deliver the same (or an increased) scope of service.

The rest of this book considers these dimensions and the three-dimensional 'Cube' that they form. In the years to come, all corporations—big and small—will have to find their way through this three-dimensional space. It will not be an easy journey, particularly for the giant corporations born of the very different ways of the twentieth century. Throughout the book we offer suggestions that we hope will help both the lost and the lonely on their way.

3

The Cube Route to Survival

I N CHAPTER 1 WE LOOKED AT THE REMARKABLE WAY IN which the twentieth century was the century of the large corporation, a time when most of the economic, social and political advantages lay with large companies rather than with small ones. Then in Chapter 2 we looked at the no less remarkable way in which, at the end of the twentieth century, many of these advantages were worn away.

So where has that left those organisations that grew up on the twentieth-century premise that to be big was to be impregnable? It has certainly left them fearful and floundering. But those that take the pains to understand the environment in which they are living, and the ways in which it is changing, can begin to find a way through to a promising future for themselves and for all those that work with them.

For the changes that are taking place are not such that they imply that large firms must necessarily die. They do not constitute a cataclysmic climatic change like that which probably brought about the end of the dinosaurs. Rather, the changes are more like global warming, something that allows time for creatures to adapt, for birds to migrate further north, for example.

The one thing it does not allow them to do, however, is to stay still. They have to keep moving, and they will need a

good deal of skilled management if they are to navigate
successfully through the changes that I have described so
far. There are few simple prescriptions. Firms will need to
keep a look out in many different directions at once and to
alter their course according to their circumstances.

Three dimensions

For a large corporation to survive and thrive it is sure to have
to make fundamental changes in three areas or dimensions:

1. The nature of what they offer to their customers.
2. The business model—i.e. the nature of the
    relationship they have with their customers.
3. The level of virtualisation—i.e. the extent to which
    a firm tries to do everything itself, or works with
    third parties to deliver the same (or an increased)
    scope of service.

These dimensions can be thought of as the bounds of a
three-dimensional space in which businesses will have to
move in the twenty-first century. All businesses have to
think immediately about how they can best move from the
bottom left-hand front corner of this space (which is where
most of them are now) and in a generally upward and
onward direction.

The three axes in Figure 3.1 reflect ways of doing
business that I can envisage with reasonable clarity today.
In an earlier book (*Destination Z: The History of the
Future*) I set out a framework for thinking about a future
that lies well beyond the furthest point on these axes. But

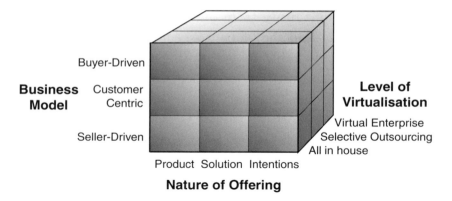

Figure 3.1   The cube route to success

here my aim is to help firms identify what they can practically try to achieve now and in the next few years.

Each of the three dimensions in the model can be divided roughly into three separate stages:

✦ The first stage is where most companies stand today and represents the business reality for most of the twentieth century.
✦ The second stage is about as far as today's most innovative companies have reached.
✦ The third stage is the point to which companies that want to remain successful well into the twenty-first century need to drive themselves towards.

At any particular moment in its history, every organisation can be located within this three-dimensional space. Its position represents the extent to which it is an organisation suited for the twentieth century or one suited for the twenty-first.

Organisations move from one point to another as their nature changes. And they have to keep on moving because if they feel comfortable in one position for too long then that spot soon becomes overcrowded. It will be occupied by a large number of competitors, also keen to enjoy the comfort that your organisation has evidently found there. These competitors, however, have sharp elbows and they will ungraciously push the incumbents out. For those pushed out, there is no guarantee of a soft landing.

The first dimension

The first dimension of our cube represents what's on offer to consumers in the marketplace. It begins with the traditional 'product', a thing that is (literally) produced by a corporation in the hope that it will catch a customer's eye and meet someone's need somewhere. Products (and the same applies to services) are developed by firms internally, driven by inward-looking R&D, and focused on attracting buyers through their price and 'features' (things like leather interiors in a car, for instance, or individual TV screens on the backs of airline seats).

A classic product or service-based organisation has all the complication and expense of keeping stock and trying to judge demand. It encourages firms to organise themselves in a series of product-related vertical 'silos'. The loyalty of employees is to others up and down the same silo, which may not be in the customer's best interest.

Some organisations are looking to go beyond this and to package a number of products and services together in order to make life easier for their customers. Thus the supermarket puts the pasta sauces next to the pasta and the

Parmesan cheese; the travel company sells travel insurance and anti-malaria pills as well as a packaged tour.

Such companies are seeking to provide 'solutions' for customers rather than simple products. They are trying to help consumers to solve problems, like 'What shall I eat for dinner tonight?' instead of simply enabling them to buy a series of products independently—meat, carrots, potatoes, etc.—and create their own solution. The massive growth of sales in semi-frozen pre-prepared meals in western supermarkets in recent years has shown how eager customers can be to buy 'solutions'.

Car manufacturers are also moving towards providing solutions. Cars nowadays are sold less on style and the size of their wing-fins than on the function they are required to perform. If you need a vehicle that can regularly take you, your partner, three children, two dogs and one mother-in-law to the seaside on Sundays, then there are a number of vehicles designed to provide a solution to your 'problem'. Likewise if you just need a vehicle to take you and your partner around town in style then there is a different range of vehicles designed just for you.

Further along this dimension, beyond solutions, lie what I call 'Intentions'. Here I am not talking about intentions in the everyday sense of the word—I am talking about fundamental and wide personal goals that many of us share. These Intentions direct our lives and determine many of the things that we do and buy. They include goals like 'a comfortable old age' or 'a good education for the children'.

As well as broad intentions like these, people also have narrower 'sub-intentions'. In order to secure a comfortable old age, for example, people need to find a suitable home, to achieve a certain level of financial security, or to maintain a healthy lifestyle. Each of these in itself is a sort of intention.

Satisfying intentions of the broad or narrow variety requires putting together a customised package of solutions, each of which in turn consists of a package of products and services. So it soon becomes clear that an organisation that is trusted by consumers to satisfy their intentions is going to be in a position to sell them an awful lot of goods and services.

To see all these different levels more clearly, consider the business of travel. Travel broadens the mind and as such it could have a place in someone's intention to give their children a good education. It could also be part of someone's intention to have a comfortable old age. They might feel that they could not be old and happy had they not seen, for instance, Venice or San Francisco before they were incapable of making the journey.

At the moment there is a wide range of travel products and services for sale that we can assemble for ourselves in order to provide solutions to the problem, 'Where to go on holiday this year'. We can buy a train ticket or an airline ticket, book a hotel room and rent a car. Alternatively we can go to a tour operator who sells us a pre-packaged service. The service will include travel and hotel and various add-ons, and it might provide a solution to our holiday problem. But it will not have been customised to such an extent that it does not involve the purchaser in making some compromises. Maybe we cannot get the room with a sea view that we really desire, or a flight that is not in the middle of the night.

One step on from this are companies like American Express which are trying to provide customised 'solutions' to consumers' problems in the sense that I refer to in the cube. A customer might call American Express and say he wants to go to Milan from New York via Vienna; he then wants to spend a weekend by the shores of Lake Maggiore before driving on to Geneva and flying back to New York. American Express is able to draw on the expertise of different parts of its business to arrange a seamless 'packaged' holiday that is tailored to the customer's exact requirements.

What sort of business will be able to persuade consumers that it can help them to fulfil their intentions, package solutions so that their broadest lifetime goals are fulfilled? First of all it is going to be an organisation that establishes a completely new sort of relationship with its customers, a much closer and more intimate relationship. There will have to be an almost continuous two-way learning process between the business and the customer.

Customers will have to feed their financial and personal details into an electronic database so that producers know what they should offer them. Only that way can producers hope to be able to monitor customers' changing circumstances and to judge when to make another step towards satisfying their intentions—to know, for example, when they might want to change their car because their children have finished university and left home.

Although such close relationships between consumer and provider do not yet exist, there are some examples of how markets are moving in that direction. A Web-based business called Third Age (Figure 3.2), for example, collects information from individuals who are in the so-called 'third age' of their lives, the stage where their children have left home. It then targets products and services that might be of

Third Age Profile

Characteristic	Details
Customer	• Individual and empty nesters families looking for a simple way to manage and delegate financial, lifestyle, health and daily logistics challenges
Customer Strategy	• Trusted agent providing buyers with comprehensive offering, individually tailored and spanning multiple industries, connecting with others of like interest
Market • Segments	• High-service customers willing to delegate tasks
• Brand	• Start-up Web-site building a name in community of buyers
Selling • Product/ Service features	• "For mature adults" - services for adults over age 45: - travel planning and execution - managing finances, investments and estate issues - maintaining health and fitness
• Price	• Free access to chat rooms and information • Buying power of the integrator vs. providers enhanced by the growing number of community members
• Channels	• On-line
Service	• Access to community buyers of like interest • Network of accredited providers

Figure 3.2   The Third Age profile. (Reproduced by permission of Third Age.)

specific interest to such a consumer group—things like nutritional products, and leisure and health services. These are then delivered through a network of partners that includes the online brokerage firm E*Trade, the electronic florist 1-800-Flowers, and Toys 'R' Us (for the 'first age' grandchildren, presumably).

The second dimension

Along the second dimension of our cube lie changes in the business model, in the ways in which markets operate. In today's business world markets are fundamentally seller-driven. The only things for sale are produced by firms whose value propositions are based on a combination of price and service. Products are manufactured with particular customer segments in mind and then 'push' marketed, often through several channels. Such seller-driven firms carry a large proportion of unprofitable customers, and they fail to make the most of opportunities presented by those customers who are profitable. Typical UK banks, for example, only realise a profit from 40% or less of their customers; with some banks this figure is as low as 20%! The problem that seller-driven banks face in current times is summarised in Figure 3.3.

The standard business today is built around products and services. Each product or service group is built around its own divisions, such as development, manufacturing and marketing, even if that replicates what is going on elsewhere in the business. It may also have its own finance staff and its own IT staff. In this vertical structure, each product or service group is like a functional 'silo'. There is little co-ordination of the activities of one silo with those of any

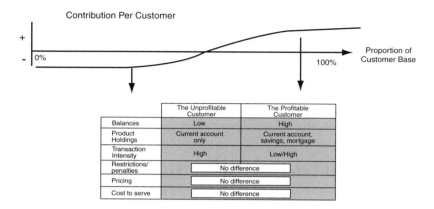

Figure 3.3   Contribution per customer

other and, to all intents and purposes, each product's silo might as well be a separate company. This is the essence of the seller-driven model. No one with any sense would ever design a business this way —it's just how they have evolved.

In particular, each product silo pushes its output to its own customers, regardless of what any of the other silos might be doing. This completely wastes any opportunities for cross-selling and leads to widespread inefficiency. Bank customers, for instance, frequently receive promotional material from one department of the bank at about the same time as they receive similar material from another arm of the same bank. One of the most popular sayings among consumers today is that the left arm doesn't seem to know what the right arm is doing.

As Kate Harmon, from Andersen Consulting, wrote recently:

> *'The loyalty and commitment that employees feel toward*

their managers and functional fiefdoms adversely affects customer service. Employees look up to their managers instead of out for their customers. The desire to out-perform a rival function within the company overshadows the needs and wants of the customer.'

New entrants can avoid some of these structural faults. Virgin Direct, founded in 1995 as a joint venture between Virgin and the Norwich Union insurance company, had the luxury, said its managing director Rowan Gormley, of 'moulding the company to the customer, not the other way round'. That meant that it was able to develop a more fluid and horizontal structure.

Virgin Direct had the great advantage of starting from scratch. For firms built in the traditional way to turn themselves around is not easy. Oticon, a Swedish hearing-aid manufacturer, found that its attempts to change its organisational structure, incentive schemes and job descriptions became overwhelming and took far longer than it expected. Lars Kolind, the man behind the changes, said the reason was:

'We are not in the business of creating innovative organisations. Our work is about developing the world's best hearing care.'

To become more customer-centric, firms will have to break out of their old product-oriented silo-shaped mould. They will have to become horizontal organisations that cut across product boundaries in order to package solutions for their customers. Their organisational structure will have to be built to service customers, not themselves.

Technology is now driving us towards markets which

are entirely controlled by consumers who dictate what they want and invite producers to supply them—a frightening prospect for the seller-driven firms. Firms that wish to meet the challenges of this market will have to become radically different. Customer segments, for instance, will be segments of one. It will not be enough that organisations restructure themselves in more customer-centric ways. The process of mass customisation that lay behind the customer-centric firm, the production of large volumes of personalised products by the use of standardised 'platforms', will not be enough for the buyer-driven market.

In such a market there is no easy way of anticipating in advance what the customer wants. Buyers will not go from shop to shop hunting for the items that they want. They will send their shopping lists to an intermediary whom they trust, and the intermediary will invite firms to bid for the business. The whole system will be dependent on the ease and speed with which it will be possible to disseminate information from any one individual on the face of the earth to any other.

The combination of the technologies of the mobile phone and the miniaturised computer will bring sellers, intermediaries and buyers into a new sort of relationship in which information will be continuously exchanged between them. Producers will be helped by so-called 'collaborative technologies', such as wireless broadband communications, real-time data access and business simulation—technologies that will make it easier to share information across enterprises. Manufacturers will thus be able to work together speedily to make bids that match up to customers' demands.

The third dimension

Along the third dimension of change in our three-dimensional cube lies the nature of the organisation itself. This is undergoing a dramatic upheaval from the type of organisation where everything was done in-house to the type of organisation where very little is done in-house. The latter, generally referred to as a 'virtual enterprise', is exemplified by firms like Richard Branson's Virgin Cola and the Visa International payment-card operation.

With the benefit of hindsight, it seems extraordinary that firms should have persisted throughout the twentieth century in doing everything for themselves. There are so many examples of firms that have either reduced costs as a result of outsourcing some functions, and/or strengthened their hand as a result of forming an alliance with a company that had a better product than the home-grown version, for example. But it was so important to the typical twentieth century firm to have control over all aspects of their operation that most firms kept everything pretty much in-house.

There were always a few notable exceptions to this. Advertising was one, catering, another. These tasks were traditionally for many years outsourced to third party suppliers. What has happened in recent years is a dramatic extension of the range of functions and processes that firms have seen fit to outsource, and a shift in the way that they have done the outsourcing.

It all began with information technology and a realisation by organisations that here was something that by its very nature was not suited to being done in-house. Firms could not keep abreast of the changes in new technology and the continual demand for new bits of hardware and software. Here at last was something that general managers were forced to admit was beyond their comprehension.

Moreover, IT required a different management culture from that of the organisation which made use of it. In the early days of IBM mainframes, the boffins who ran them were treated like R&D scientists, given white coats and shut away in basements. But in time they came to realise that although they were being treated like lunatics they were in fact running the asylum. Their area of responsibility was central to the organisations that they worked for. So the best of them left in order to run their own businesses, and to see some more natural light.

A lot of other in-house IT staff moved for a slightly different reason. It became a common feature of IT outsourcing contracts that the outsourcer took on the IT staff of the organisation whose IT it was going to develop and run. Many of the staff were happy to move to a firm which understood the special needs of their line of business, and which was able to provide far more opportunities for future career development.

For most firms, outsourcing is still a selective process in which a fairly narrow and defined range of functions is seen as suitable for outsourcing. Most of these are related to IT, and they range from the low ground of basic PC network management to the higher ground of IT strategy and implementation. Other areas to which the outsourcing idea is spreading include marketing and finance.

Meanwhile, the nature of the outsourcing contract itself has been changing. In many cases it has moved on from being a straightforward contract between a buyer and a supplier of services to become more like a strategic alliance in which both parties share the risks and rewards of the outsourced activity. This is exactly what happened at AMP, the Australian insurance company, that formed a joint venture called AMPlus, an arm's length IT company owned by AMP but run by Andersen Consulting.

Alliances are set to become a much more important part of the corporate landscape. In a joint study with the Economist Intelligence Unit, Andersen Consulting asked senior executives how important alliances with other firms in the same industry were for their business. While 17% said they thought that they were important today, 36% said that they thought they would be crucial in 10 years' time.

I believe that alliances will become a necessary part of doing business in the twenty-first century for two main reasons:

1. The quickest and cheapest way for a company to enter a new market space where it does not have the necessary competencies and/or credentials is by teaming with an organisation that does. This is precisely the path that the UK supermarkets have taken to enter financial services in the UK. They have all formed alliances with an existing bank.

    Initially, they tried to link up with the traditional English 'high street' banks, big institutions like NatWest which have control of a large part of the financial-services business in England. But these institutions soon found the threat of the supermarkets too much to handle. So the supermarkets turned to the Scottish banks instead, a group which had traditionally not attempted to penetrate the market south of the Scottish border. And since then this business has grown into a lucrative new revenue stream for the Scottish banks.

2.   Companies can increase their attractiveness to their customers by either 'abandoning' some of their home-grown, poor performing products in place of ones provided by third parties, or by complementing their home-grown products with those of third parties. It is this latter path which Charles Schwab has followed with such success in the twentieth century.

Taken to their extreme, strategic alliances lead to the virtual enterprise—the enterprise which links with others in order to provide a total service while doing 'very little' of the work themselves. In such firms almost everything is outsourced. In the classic example of Richard Branson's Virgin organisation, Virgin Cola, Virgin financial products and Virgin trains are all virtual organisations. Virgin owns neither bottling plants nor banks nor railway carriages. Through networks of alliances it organises others to produce the goods and services on which it stamps its brand.

Visa, the credit-card outfit, is also a virtual organisation. Although Visa is thought of as one of the biggest card-issuing companies in the world, with its name appearing on at least 600 million cards from Saigon to Santiago, the San Francisco-based organisation does not actually offer cards or financial services directly itself. That is carried out by its members, the 21,000 financial institutions around the world that actually issue the Visa cards.

Visa itself consists of five regional offices located around the world, in addition to the San Francisco office, each of them with a relatively small staff and few fixed assets.

The organisation provides telecommunications links for its branded card system and handles the processing of payments. Most importantly, it sets operating standards that ensure the consistency and quality of the services that carry its name. That puts it into a position where it is able to protect its most valuable asset: its brand.

Visa also provides a sort of R&D function for its members, taking them into the next century through its development of the 'smart card', the plastic card with an embedded electronic chip, and through its leadership in setting standards of security for Internet transactions.

Its acknowledgement of the significance of the Internet, where it has formed a close alliance with Yahoo!, one of the best-known Internet 'portals', gave the whole idea of eCommerce a big boost. In a deal signed at the end of 1997, Visa took a small 2% stake in Yahoo! and the two organisations jointly agreed to set up a comprehensive Web-shopping guide. Visa agreed to advertise extensively on the Yahoo! site while Yahoo! designated Visa as its preferred credit card. The two companies are also collaborating on a data-privacy standard for secure electronic transactions (called SET).

I believe that as we enter a new economy for a new millennium, it is essential that businesses relate their current position to the three dimensions I have described. Then, once a firm has established where it stands now, it can use these dimensions to guide it on its journey into the future. In the chapters ahead I will explain each of them in more detail.

4

Dimension One— Changing offerings

For much of the twentieth century, industrial society was organised around products and services, not customers. Discrete products were sold through physical distribution channels to undifferentiated clientele. A current account was a current account was a current account, regardless of whether the customer was a member of the Rockerfeller family or a sharecropper from the Mid-West.

Occasionally consumers were lucky, and they found that they had a choice. With things like white goods, for example, sometimes they could choose a big size, and sometimes they could choose a small size. But whichever size they chose, the products were almost guaranteed to be an eyesore in every kitchen where they came to rest. Manufacturers did not attempt to take into account variations in taste and style. They just assumed that their output was bound for identikit homes in endless rows of ribbon development or in soaring towers of block-solid apartments.

The consumers who tolerated these mass produced, impersonal products did not fool themselves that they were spoilt for choice. The reason that they did not protest probably lay in their recent history. For most of the century, the consumer's mind-set was framed by widespread shortages—the shortages of the First World War and its immediate aftermath; the shortages of the Depression and of the era of European hyper-inflation; and then the terrible deprivation of the Second World War. Economies in such times are inevitably driven by supply, not demand—by the producers of goods, not the consumers of them. Consumers took whatever was on offer, and by and large they were grateful.

Large corporations were also grateful. Low consumer expectations helped them to get on with the job of running things for their own benefit. In *The Changing Anatomy of Britain*, Anthony Sampson wrote of the UK in the late 1960s:

> At the peak of the corporate state, [the creation of] giant companies [by merger] made planning and negotiation simpler for everyone, with no tiresome complications about efficiency or consumer choice to get in the way.

Those days, however, are long since gone, though traces remain in the memory of older members of the 'baby-boom' generation in Europe. They can still remember the rationing of a range of everyday goods (like sugar and petrol) that followed the Second World War. But that mind-set is on its way out. For the large majority of consumers today, supply is not (and never has been) an issue. They feel empowered in a way that previous generations never did. And that feeling is becoming so strong that it is driving large corporations everywhere to think again about the basic business model that has served them so well in the past, in some cases for more than a century.

The phrase 'The customer is king' has been in common parlance for so long that people have come to believe that it has been true for years. But it hasn't. If anyone was king in the recent past, it was the producer. The customer was merely an afterthought, an undifferentiated set of arms and legs that was going to be lucky enough to pay for the wonderful products that were being produced by wonderful corporations. It is only very recently that such attitudes have begun to change.

The famous quotation from the advertising pioneer David Ogilvie: 'The consumer is not a moron; she is your wife', sounds slightly absurd today. Who, at the beginning of the twenty-first century, would dare to take the consumer for a moron? But at the time when it first appeared (in a book published in 1963), the comment was eye opening. Corporations then did often take the public for fools, lavishing generous perks on their own managers largely at the expense of the consumer.

For most people, the way this worked was ill understood. But literature occasionally acknowledged the process. In *Murder Must Advertise*, written by Dorothy L. Sayers in 1933, one of her characters says,

> *By forcing the damn fool public to pay twice over—once to have its food emasculated and once to have the vitality put back again—we keep the wheels of commerce turning.*

The public, Sayers' characters agreed, was a damn fool. It is perhaps not surprising that when the tables were turned in favour of consumers, their distaste for big business was deeply ingrained.

The best that could be said of large corporations was

that they were patronising. And on occasions they were far worse than that. The revelations of the American car industry's scant regard for consumer safety in the 1960s and 1970s became a watershed in the relationship between consumers and producers. Similarly, the current redefining of the tobacco companies' responsibility for the health of their customers is taking the relationship into yet new territory. It is territory, however, where the consumer sits firmly on the throne.

Misplaced loyalty

Corporations were slow to feel the winds of change because many of them were able to fool themselves that the public was happy with the way that things were. Car manufacturers, for instance, thought they had a very satisfied band of customers because people went out and bought the same brand of car again and again.

But that often had more to do with the way that cars were sold than with the cars themselves. It was just so much easier for consumers to revisit the same car dealer—who only sold the one brand, and who gave them the best price for their old vehicle. Firms like General Motors thrived for years on this sort of customer inertia, which they mistakenly interpreted as loyalty.

Even when Japanese manufacturers began to break into the American and European car markets and to cause a major disturbance in the 1980s, they did so without overturning the existing distribution systems. They adapted them to suit their own purposes, not the consumer's.

At the time, Japanese companies were beginning to compete with the biggest and the best manufacturers in many industries across the world. But they competed with them to provide better products; they did not compete with them to provide better value to consumers or greater convenience. Japan's own inefficient distribution system shows what little concern its industry has had by and large for the consumer, be that consumer Japanese or foreign. Large Japanese corporations, already under tremendous pressure from the structural ills of the Japanese economy, are going to have as hard a time as any in adjusting to the new customer-centric world.

Many financial-service firms were also lulled at this time into believing that they had a loyal band of customers. After all, whole families would stay with the same bank, generation after generation. Few banks stopped to wonder whether that was the positive attribute of loyalty or the negative attribute of inertia.

In many cases, of course, it was the latter. The costs of financial services like banking, insurance and stockbroking have rarely been transparent, and consumers have always had a hard time comparing the cost of one provider's services with those of another. This has been the breeding ground of many a financial scandal.

Governments have sometimes intervened to give the consumer greater protection against the sharks swimming in their waters. In banking, the introduction in the UK of the legal requirement to show the APR (annualised percentage rate) of all loan products is one example of an attempt to frustrate the unscrupulous.

With insurance and stockbroking, the potential to confuse the average consumer has been even greater. Many people have come to realise too late that they are committed to paying enormous commissions for insurance policies that they have bought through agents whom they had engaged to tell them which was the best policy for them. The 'best' policy too frequently turned out to be the one with the highest commission for the agent.

As soon as someone came along who was able to offer Joe Public an escape from the ties that bound him to using such agents, he embraced them with great enthusiasm. Direct selling of insurance products by telephone, for instance, took off like a rocket and revolutionised the market in several countries during the 1990s. In the UK, a company called Direct Line, a newcomer to the business, used the increasing sophistication of telecommunications services to steal market share from the traditional providers. Scarcely any of them was subsequently able to resist following Direct Line's example.

The consumer's escape from the stockbrokers' cartel (their fixed commission structure), and the brokers' in-built tendency to 'churn' any customer's portfolio, has come with yet another technological development—the introduction of electronic trading via the Internet. Online discount brokers and newcomers like E*Trade rewrote the rules of that particular game and gave consumers a new low-cost structure.

Ironically, it also made many individuals churn their portfolios at a rate that would have embarrassed even the greediest broker in the bad old days. The rise of these so-called 'day traders' in the United States has added a powerfully bullish element to financial markets in recent years.

The customer fights back

The 1990s was the decade when consumers finally began to show their dissatisfaction with the manufacturers' product-oriented vision. Industrial society reached a stage where supply was definitely no longer the issue. In most sectors there were enough suppliers for customers to have real choices at last. And as competition made those customers more and more aware of price differentials, they looked increasingly for 'value for money'. Indeed, the 1990s have already been described as 'the decade of value'.

This was taking place at the same time as greater competition among suppliers was leading to the 'commoditisation' of a large number of goods and services. Competing manufacturers' products were becoming indistinguishable in many respects. Kitchenware looked the same everywhere; bathtubs too. And their price was more or less the same.

Customers became far less interested in products *per se*. What they were looking for was the value that came as an add-on to the product. The general process of commoditisation taking place in most markets led them to look elsewhere than the product itself for value. In such an environment, the sort of value that consumers were seeking for their money became much more intangible.

Value came to embrace all sorts of things, like convenience and simplicity, for instance. Consumers became increasingly impatient with any form of waiting. Surveys invariably find that the *bête noir* in most consumers' shopping experience is 'queuing at the check-out'. Nowadays time is of the essence.

Regis McKenna, the marketing guru from California

who spawned the idea of relationship marketing, says that what customers today want most from a product 'is often qualitative and intangible: it is the benefit and service that is integral to the product. Service is not an event; it is the process of creating a customer environment of information, assurance and comfort.'

This reflects the widening realisation that products are but a small part of what most customers want. In the 1990s, those companies that became aware of the changing dynamics between supplier and consumer came to realise that they were going to have to shift their effort away from the production of tangible objects. Satisfying and retaining customers was going to be all about providing qualitative intangible things, things that—to quote Bishop Berkeley—'have not any subsistence without a mind'.

And a number of firms have enjoyed great success by shifting their focus to intangibles—firms like the American department store Nordstrom, for example, whose staff are now encouraged to ring customers when something has just come into the store that they think might interest them.

Original as Nordstrom would like to think that its policy is, it is only another example of the way that business life tends to repeat itself. In the nineteenth and early twentieth century, milliners and dressmakers around the world would offer a similar style of service to Nordstrom's, informing all their regular customers when the 'latest collections' had arrived. And the milkman at the time might have delivered extra eggs to Mrs Smith when he knew that Mrs Smith's hungry nephews had come to stay. Such service has existed before; it's just that it's been quiescent for several decades.

Intangibles can be even less tangible than Nordstrom's.

They may lie in the courier firm, for instance, which trains its agents to make sure that their visits are seen as a pleasant break, not an inconvenient interruption. Or they may lie in a busy post office where polite efficiency seems to overcome all problems.

Increasingly, of course, they do not even involve the visual senses. The telephone is becoming more and more important as an interface between consumers and producers. People nowadays receive so many direct sales approaches by phone that they can tell within a few seconds whether the caller has the sort of approach that is likely to make them interested—almost regardless of the product or service that is being sold to them.

Jan Carlzon, a former CEO of Scandinavian Airlines Systems (SAS), wrote in his book, *Moments of Truth*, (Harper Collins, 1989), that

> *the essence of any organisation is communicated in the single fleeting moment when someone in that organisation connects with a customer. This communication takes place, for example, when a flight attendant brings you your coffee, a receptionist bids you good morning, or a salesperson calls to tell you your order has arrived. Taken together, these small, seemingly inconsequential moments define who you are and establish your worth in the marketplace. The greater the number of positive moments you have, the greater the value of your enterprise.*

What these intangible things do is to provide something extra for the consumer, something that stretches products and services beyond their fundamental face value. The direction in which they are to be stretched in the future is to be determined by the consumer. And it will be the direction in which those products and services can do most to solve the typical time-hungry person's everyday problems—things like making their travel arrangements, preserving their wealth, and feeding their families.

Large firms accustomed to selling products to inert buyers (for as large a margin as they can command) need to reconfigure themselves in order to focus single-mindedly on providing solutions to the problems of the active consumers. That will lead remorselessly, as William A. Band wrote in *Touchstones* (John Wiley, 1994), to a world where 'the paradigm of doing business will shift from making a product to providing a service'. In the few years since that was written, the paradigm has already shifted. Successful firms today are focused primarily on providing a service.

Convenience

Let's look more closely at the nature of this service, at the things that add value to the consumers' buying experience and for which they are prepared to pay a price. At the top of the list undoubtedly comes convenience. In at least one industry, grocery retailing, convenience has already come to the consumer in big doses. In the 1950s, a housewife doing her weekend shopping would have to visit half a dozen shops in order to buy food, cleaning materials and other household products. She would gain a sort of value from doing that—in terms of the relationships that she would establish in her community, and in terms of the information that she would glean in the process—but none of that value would be immediately convertible into cash.

Cash, for the housewife of the 1950s and 1960s,

increasingly came from going out to work, and going out to work left her less time to go shopping. Pioneering stores realised this, stores like Wal-Mart in the United States and Tesco and Sainsbury in the UK, and they opened supermarkets, assembling all the goods on a typical household's weekly shopping list under one roof for the convenience of the increasingly hurried consumer.

The drive to provide greater convenience within supermarkets has been continuous. Successful firms realise that there is no let up. There is no one level of convenience that can be called perfect. Technology and competition are always changing the goalposts.

At first, shoppers had no choice but to do their household shopping on a Saturday or during working hours. Now, however, they can find supermarkets that are open until late in the evening, and supermarkets that are open all day on Sunday. In a growing number of places people can even find ones that are open all night.

Then again, sophisticated tracking systems have recently enabled stores to determine how many customers are in the store at any one time. They can thus work out how many checkout points will be needed in ten minutes' time. This has given a new focus to competition: the speed at which shoppers can be processed at the checkout points.

Stores also involved in a continuous attempt to make their lay-outs more attractive and convenient to customers, putting the tomato sauces next to the pasta, for instance, and the mint sauces next to the lamb, rather than 12 aisles away with the rest of the sauces.

In some industries, however, the levels of convenience are still stuck in the prehistoric age. For example, consumers still have to use a dozen different suppliers to provide them with household services. They need one firm to provide a plumber, another for an electrician, another to fix the gas, another to clean the windows, and so on.

Imagine if there were household services supermarkets which you could ring up one day and say: 'I need a plumber to clear a blocked drain. And whilst you're in the house could you clean the windows and adjust the television aerial. Channel X has not been clear since they built that new office block down the road. My partner will be in the house between 10 and 12 and I'll be there after 5. Come between those hours please.' Sounds like bliss? Well, it may be closer than you think.

Trust

The value of convenience is followed by the value of things like simplicity and safety and trust. Consumers want to buy from someone that they believe is committed to providing them with value for money. In a supermarket they want to be able to believe that the prices are more or less competitive with everybody else's. And they want to trust the quality of the produce that they are buying. They do not want to spend valuable time worrying about having been overcharged or wondering whether it's normal for lamb chops to smell that way.

Steve Jobs, whose Apple computer company first popularised the PC, once played cleverly on this need for trust in his battle to convert consumers from the culture of the mainframe. Apple's advertising slogan at the time was, 'Never trust a computer you can't lift'.

Trust is particularly important with something like household services. You don't want any old Tom, Dick or

Harry wandering round your house cleaning the windows or checking for a gas leak. You want to feel that you can leave whoever it is to get on with the job. Otherwise it becomes very time-consuming if you have to clear away everything valuable before the service agent arrives, or follow him around like a private detective all the time he's there.

The traditional way of fostering trust in a product-based world is by branding, by building up the reputation of a particular product's name so that customers feel warmly towards it and want to buy it again . . . and again. And there is no doubt that powerful brands can command an extraordinary degree of trust. A survey by the UK's Henley Centre ('Planning for Social Change', 1998), for example, found that in the UK top brands like Kellogg's, Cadbury's, Heinz and Nescafé are trusted 'to be honest and fair' much more than are individuals' banks, the church, the police, or their Member of Parliament. The only pillar of the establishment that beat all consumer brands was the GP, the local doctor. Consumers, it seems, are still prepared to trust their doctor with their life.

In the value-conscious 1990s, some firms began to stretch their brands beyond their products so that they came to embrace the intangibles that consumers had started to value so highly. One organisation at the forefront of this process was Richard Branson's Virgin group in the UK. It has stretched its brand beyond music shops and airlines and taken it into an area of general trust. Consumers first of all trust Richard Branson, despite the fact that he persists in risking his life in hot air balloons and the like. They then trust his company (i.e. Virgin) and from there, go on to bestow their trust on anything that carries the Virgin name.

The nature of the trust that people bestow on intangibles means that even if aspects of a product or service are temporarily disappointing, the trust can remain. At times Virgin's rail service, for example, has been far from excellent—indeed, on many measures, it has been worse than it was under the state-owned enterprise which ran the railway previously. But customers fail to direct the same anger at Virgin because they genuinely believe that it is concerned about trying hard to improve the service for their benefit.

The big danger for a brand like Virgin is that it becomes too closely connected with a single individual. Other value-based brands are in a similar position—Dell with Michael Dell, and The Body Shop with Anita Roddick. What happens when the individuals behind the names move on, or turn out to be something other than their carefully cultivated image?

Simplicity

The consumer's demand for simplicity is best demonstrated by the demand for information. It is not more information that people want, by and large. It is simplification of the information to which they already have access—whether it be on the Internet or in a newspaper. The most popular parts of 'serious' newspapers like the *Wall Street Journal* and the *Financial Times*, for example, are often the digests on the front page. Many busy people judge their papers largely on that, and a wise publication puts its best people onto what has traditionally been considered a menial task.

The popularity of books which digest information is

another indicator. Guides to restaurants, to medical information, and even guides to guides are proliferating on booksellers' shelves. And the extent of the use of search engines and bookmarks of favourite sites on the Internet is an indication of the demand among users of the World Wide Web for guidance, for an ordering and simplifying of the information that is available to them. There is not a great clamouring for more online information for its own sake. The demand is generally for less—for less pornography, fewer details about how to make bombs, etc.

This yearning for simplicity is also having an effect on traditional industries dominated by large old-fashioned organisations. A 1995 study of the US retail banking business by Andersen Consulting found that the trend towards product proliferation in US retail banking was both confusing and alienating consumers. The consultant leading the study said at the time that,

> banks would do better to offer fewer and simpler products. Many large US institutions with 12 to 15 products in credit cards would be better off with just five.

Organisations which can offer customer-centric simplicity, convenience and trust are going to be in great demand. Some companies are investing large sums in order to turn themselves into something which can provide such values. For example, America's two biggest long-distance telephone companies, AT&T and MCI, have joined together in a digital satellite broadcasting venture. The satellite can beam into people's homes both entertainment (via the television) and data (via the computer and the telephone). The idea is that the same company (AT&T or MCI) will be able to provide the customer with telephone, television and computer services. The name of the game is simplicity: one provider, one bill and one repairman.

The drivers of change

The intangible things that consumers have come to value have been determined to a large extent by their changing lifestyle, and lifestyles today are changing faster than ever before. So, therefore, are the things that consumers value. Any organisation that wants to be in the business of adding value to consumers in the future has to have a deep understanding of where those consumers are coming from.

Fundamental to all changes in lifestyle is the change in the nature of the family. And one of the major changes there in recent years has been the sharp rise in the number of family units in which both partners are working. This has been a key driver of the demand for convenience, and of the changing nature of the shopping 'experience'.

When they are not working, these people want to relax, and they are prepared to pay others to do the tasks which their housewife mothers in their day used to do for their family units. Hence there has been a vast growth in the number of firms providing cleaning services (for cars, clothes and homes); in the number of restaurants and of other providers of 'convenience foods'; and in the number of crèches and child-minding services.

Some of these services are bought by the employers of these double-income families rather than by individuals themselves. A growing number of companies, for instance, provide child-care facilities at their employees' place of work. Some of them even provide a sort of 'super-valet' service for their employees, a number of people employed specifically to see to the personal needs of other employees—buying birthday presents on their behalf, for example, or booking a plumber, or finding the time of a convenient flight.

Others are making a business out of this demand. In the United States in particular there has been a rapid growth in recent years of firms providing companies with what are called corporate concierge services. Services vary from booking restaurants, to finding cleaners and checking out accommodation. It can even stretch to creating a social life for an executive whose work may force him or her to change cities every six months. This is increasingly common in consulting-type services where employees may work in one place during the week and then fly back to a completely different city for the weekends, the city where their partners and children live.

Look at this extract from the *Wall Street Journal* of 26 April 1999:

It didn't take long for Juan Meija to realise that trying to find an apartment in Manhattan was incompatible with working up to 75 hours a week. After several months of living at the World Trade Center Marriott last summer, Mr Meija, a software consultant at PeopleSoft, decided it was time to put down roots. His client, Goldman Sachs, had told him to plan on being in New York for at least six months for the back-office software project he was working on, but that it could take longer. So, Mr Meija turned proactive. But it quickly became apparent that a few stolen moments of glancing at the Village Voice housing listings wasn't going to cut it. 'I'd try to look at apartments during lunch . . . it almost seemed like I could have done it full-time', he says. Adding to the struggle, Saturday apartment hunting wasn't an option, since Mr Meija was flying home to Washington D.C. every weekend.

Welcome to the harried, sometimes desperate world of the mobile consultant. Frequently young and ambitious, these hyper-mobile road warriors belong to a new class of business traveler that change cities every six months and work schedules so tightly strung that they don't have time to do laundry or pay their bills.

These high earning 'road warriors'—men and women with no time to do their laundry—are one group looking for convenience and willing to pay for it. There are others too, arising from slightly different demographic shifts. For instance, one big change occurring in western societies is in the size of family units. The average size of households in the UK has fallen from 3.4 people per household in 1951 to 2.8 in 1971 and 2.4 in 1991. It is expected to fall even further, to 2.3, by 2001.

Much of this is accounted for by single parents, the consequence of the increase in divorce and the willingness of women to bear and care for children on their own. The number of lone parent households in the UK has more or less doubled since 1980. All of them are crying out for convenience.

There is another significant change also being brought about by the increase in the divorce rate. By 2010 in the UK there will be more 'step families', family units with step children, than there will be family units where all the children are 'birth children'. This new type of family unit is sometimes referred to as 'the blended family', and blended families have some special needs.

For a start, their number fluctuates more than the normal family. Kids come and go from one blended family to another. Sometimes the blended family can be seven or eight in a group, sometimes only two. At the very least that makes for wide variation in their food bills and in their transport requirements. The life of the blended family is more complicated than average and is in dire need of someone to simplify it.

Another important demographic change is in the numbers of the elderly. There has been an increase of more than 20% in the 1990s in the number of people in Europe over the age of 70 (and a 9% drop in those aged from 15–24). Not only are people living to a ripe old age way beyond their allotted three score years and ten, but they are also living with disabilities that a few generations ago they would never have survived to see. This has increased the demand for convenience from a sector of the population that is increasingly well able to pay for it—putting aside the fact that many elderly people feel moved to budget for a minimum life span of at least 150 years!

For the elderly, the intangible elements in products are probably more 'valuable' than for other sectors of the population. The elderly buy all sorts of conveniences—from nursing-home care, to taxi services, to cruise liners, to gardeners. But in anything that they buy, they value more highly the qualitative elements than an average sample of the population.

Convenience can save more time for the elderly than for the young and able-bodied; simplicity can help them more since they are more prone to be confused. And since the elderly (not without some cause) feel more vulnerable to being fleeced than the rest of us, they are more likely to persist in using brand names that they know and in dealing with salespeople that they trust.

Even if there were to be a social revolution overnight and the numbers of single-parent and double-income families were to drop dramatically, there is no way in which the numbers of the elderly could change very sharply in anything but the long term. In the meanwhile, their numbers are actually set to rise—in parallel with the demand for combinations of products and services that provide solutions to their many problems.

Solutions

In offering 'intangibles' like convenience to their customers, providers are in effect presenting them with solutions to their particular problems. With foodstuffs, for example, it is so much more 'convenient' for consumers if they can buy pre-packaged meals than it is for them to pick a bit of this, a bit of that, from a number of different retail outlets, and to combine them to create their own meal. Beyond products (i.e. foodstuffs) lie solutions (i.e. answers to questions like 'What shall we eat for dinner tonight?'). If the answer were Shepherds Pie then there would be two approaches to making this meal as shown in Figure 4.1.

The pre-preparation that is the essence of much of the value that customers are prepared to pay for can take a number of different forms. In the extreme, it comes in the form of a meal provided by a restaurant or a café. But it may be the sort of semi-chilled food pioneered in the UK by Marks & Spencer, food which is sold in meal form but which needs heating at home. Or it may just be the juxtaposition on the shelves of a supermarket of products

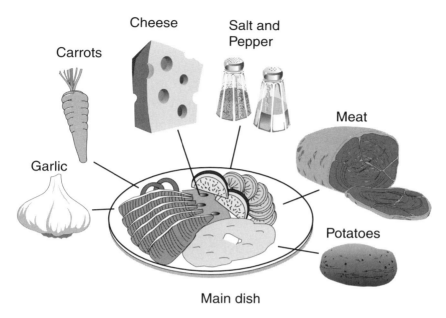

Figure 4.1 Ready-to-cook meal

that combine to make a meal. An example of the extremes of this added convenience can be largely highlighted at M&S by pre-washed salads and packets of grated cheese . . . grating cheese is by no means an arduous task yet some customers are willing to pay a premium to have it done for them.

This injection of service provides firms with a means to escape from the trap of commoditisation, a trap that is gathering ever tighter as eCommerce spreads wider. In theory, the Internet provides consumers with perfect information about products and services. This includes details about their specifications and their price, and enables consumers to make more precise choices based on price and quality.

It also means that manufacturers are never alone for long with a successful new product or service. They are copied in as much time as it takes a Xerox machine to warm up. In the fashion industry, notorious for copycats, styles and colours are now imitated so quickly that it is often difficult to discern who is the originator.

Solutions, however, provide an escape from all this. That is because a solution is not a commodity that can be replicated rapidly by anybody else in the market. It depends for its success on the uniqueness of its combination of products and services.

There are three distinctive features of solutions:

1.   **A number of products or services in more or less the same category are bundled together at the point of sale.** In financial services, for example, an institution might offer to the same customer a home loan, an insurance policy to cover the building, another policy to cover the contents, and a loan guarantee.

   Then again, a travel agent might sell a rather obvious range of things like airline tickets, hotel reservations and car hire. But he might also (at the same location) offer insurance services, travel accessories like luggage, travel guides, and even health products like anti-malaria pills and sunscreen.

2.   **The pricing of goods and services is based on the lifetime value of the customer.** Although this is presently illegal in some countries—in particular in the United States where firms cannot discriminate in the prices they charge to different customers for

the same product—it is a feature whose demands will become more pressing as firms move closer to becoming providers of solutions.

They will be under pressure to stop pricing products on the basis of the cost of their manufactured inputs, and to begin pricing them on the basis of the expected value of the solution to the customer and the expected lifetime value of that customer to the seller. Customers will be offered loss leaders aimed not just at enticing them into the store once, but at enticing them into the store for the rest of their shopping lives.

This will have an impact on employees who will have to be trained to treat all customers as if they were customers for life—in the way that they indeed were in the old days when families frequented the same butcher, baker and candlestick-maker for a generation and more. And that should set off a virtuous circle. For there is no doubt that customers who feel that they are being treated as if they were customers for life are more likely to become just that.

3. **The solutions offered to customers will increasingly be unique.** When providers bundle together products for customers they will add features and details that personalise the solution. For example, with Egg, the Prudential insurance company's new banking service, customers are able to borrow a specific amount of money over a period of their choice and to pay it back as and when they want, without penalty. With Egg's service there are far fewer of the standardised

terms and conditions, written in incomprehensible gobbledegook, that are a feature of most financial products.

Flexible manufacturing techniques are allowing a number of industries (like car manufacturers) that have traditionally turned out identikit products, to tailor their output to their customers' requirements. BMW, for instance, now boasts that there are hardly any two of its cars on the roads today that are identical. And models like the Smart car, a joint venture between the Swatch watch company and Mercedes-Benz, is turned out almost like a fashion accessory with an amazingly wide variety of colours and interior designs. The hope is that one day soon customers will buy a new little runabout almost as frequently as they buy a new outfit.

In another example, Blockbuster is working jointly on a technology that will allow customers to make their own selection of music tracks to put on a CD. Imagine turning up at a shop and saying I want a CD of this, this, this and this—all of which you heard the previous evening. And to watch it being mixed there and then onto your own personalised CD of impeccable quality. That's a solution to many people's dreams.

Know your fickle customers

A firm that wants to be in the business of providing solutions for its customers, let alone intentions, obviously needs to know those customers better than it used to. It has to be far more 'customer-centric'—a challenge I describe in more detail in the next chapter. It also has to understand that, to put it crudely, customers do not behave like they used to.

I talked in Chapter 2 about the problems that firms will face as their customers become increasingly fickle, individual and unpredictable. Christopher Field described these quirky individuals in 'The New Consumer' (published by the *Financial Times*, 1998):

> *One minute they are fastidious about their health and hygiene, only to binge the next in restaurants and curry houses. They are racked with guilt about the environment and make valiant attempts to do their bit, and will then immediately swoon over the delights of over-packaged, over-processed goods born of the labour of wage slaves living in third world dictatorships.*

Who can hope to provide solutions for such a riot of unpredictability?

One ray of hope comes from the fact that these unpredictable consumers are themselves participating in the process of providing solutions. Customers, as it were, have begun to join the supply chain. For example, consumer groups report to the general public the names of retailers which they feel are overcharging. And retailers respond. Customer questionnaires are endless and their influence on the production process is greater than it has ever been. Richard Branson claims that his Upper Class service on his Virgin airline (an upgraded business class on flights that have no first class) was the result of a passenger's suggestion. And now we hear that Richard Branson is attempting to 'put one over' on British Airways. When his arch-rival offered high-spending customers a bed on its planes, Branson offered double beds. Who came up with this suggestion I wonder?

The Internet increases these possibilities enormously. There are now sites (such as The Angry Organisation— angry.org) where people are encouraged to send in their complaints about organisations, products and services. On several occasions electronic dialogues have developed between consumer and producer that have resulted in changes to a product or service. This interface is sure to develop even further in the years to come.

Consumers have always been more loyal to providers of services than to providers of goods. Nobody changes their bank as frequently as they change their breakfast cereal (although some do change spouses more frequently than they change banks). And many people continue to stick with the same lawyers and accountants long after their experience tells them that they should have switched. (These are, perversely, the very same people who can desert a tinned-food manufacturer in droves if so much as a single insect is found in one sample of its products many thousands of miles away.)

There is a number of sound reasons why consumers are more loyal to firms that provide services. In the first place, services by definition involve an interaction between people, between the supplier and the consumer. It's much more difficult to tell your insurance agent that you're going elsewhere than it is to move along a shop shelf and take a different manufacturer's product. In many cases, too, there may be a cost in changing supplier—in passing files and personal histories from one solicitor to another, for instance, or in switching insurance policies.

In general, moreover, consumers regard buying services as more risky. So there is a greater tendency to remain loyal than there is, say, in the relatively risk-free business of purchasing baked beans.

Service will be increasingly important as firms start offering solutions rather than plain vanilla products. In the world of solutions, therefore, we can expect loyalty to be stronger. In the medium term, in a world dominated by elderly people looking for solutions, establishing loyalty is going to be absolutely vital for companies that want to be successful.

A number of companies are moving purposefully into the business of providing solutions. And some of them are coming from unlikely directions. The UK's National Westminster bank, for instance, has launched a trial service that is aimed at taking the hassle out of its customers' daily lives. Called Zenda, the service attempts to answer all sorts of customer queries, and the queries may have nothing to do with banking or finance. Recent examples include: 'How can I become a judge of pedigree dogs?'; 'Where can I rent a storm trooper costume for a Star Wars party?'; and 'Where can I find an environmentally friendly cure for pond algae?'.

If the service is successful, National Westminster intends to extend it and to offer a wedding planning service, a job search service, and a household moving service. These services will provide customers with convenience in some of the most emotionally harrowing moments of their life— arranging their wedding, finding employment and moving house—all of which involve a great sum of money, which is the food for the banks. This takes the idea of convenience way beyond provision of the evening meal. And it moves it into what Andersen Consulting call 'intentions'.

Intentions

The demands of customers will not stop with solutions. Regis McKenna, the marketing guru from California, gave his 1997 book, *Real Time*, (Harvard Business School Press, 1997), an interesting sub-title. He called it 'Preparing for the age of the never-satisfied customer'.

The never-satisfied customer will not be satisfied with solutions. He or she will look beyond meal-makers, travel organisers and other providers of short-term convenience. What these customers will want is a supplier (or a smoothly integrated network of suppliers) that can help consumers to meet their key long-term objectives in a simplified way, objectives like 'having a comfortable old age', 'maintaining a healthy lifestyle' or 'continuous personal development'.

These lifetime objectives Andersen Consulting calls 'Consumer Intentions'. And satisfying these intentions must be the aim of companies that wish to stay one step ahead of McKenna's 'never-satisfied customers' in the future. This will involve them in designing offerings that satisfy a fundamental life event or objective, something that inevitably involves extensive planning, numerous decisions and complex co-ordination.

In order to achieve their intentions in the world as it is today, consumers have to plan extensively for themselves across many areas, ranging from finance, housing and transport to healthcare, jobs and entertainment. Possible

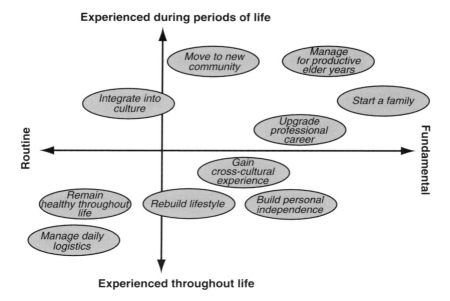

Figure 4.2   Consumer Intentions

Consumer Intentions that may be faced during one's lifetime are illustrated in Figure 4.2. To satisfy the intention of having a comfortable old age, for example, they need to draw on at least a dozen different product and service providers across several different industries. They need to make a large number of complex and time-consuming decisions, and they need to manage the process over many years.

Even a simpler intention, like maintaining a fully functioning house, requires many time-consuming decisions. Part of the enduring charm of the Jeeves stories, written by P.G. Wodehouse almost 80 years ago, lies in the innate attraction to most of us of having the perfect 'gentleman's gentleman'. The valet Jeeves deals with all the household chores of his master Bertie Wooster. He orders and watches over plumbers, electricians, gas fitters, cleaners, delivery men and other assorted service providers, and he also makes sure that their mess has been cleared up before Wooster returns.

Jeeves provides a portfolio of solutions; he solves the problem of how to mend faulty drains and of what to eat for dinner. And he also undertakes all the organisation required to get his client, Wooster, to Lower Beeding in time for the wedding of Aunt Agatha's dreary daughter. How many of us dream of having a service like that? And what would we be prepared to pay a service-provider who offered such a service (without demanding three meals a day and a bed for the night as well)?

In the world of solutions we can see how the search for intangible values is leading consumers to turn to trusted providers like Virgin or Microsoft for an ever-widening range of solutions. The idea of the trusted provider or intermediary is one that is increasingly coming to the fore, and it is one that is central to the way that I see things developing along this dimension in future. The basis on which a consumer chooses one solution provider over another is largely to do with trust.

In the world of intentions, the role of Jeeves, the intermediary service provider, becomes even more crucial than in the world of solutions. But who in the future is going to provide these intermediary services? We are, for sure, not about to see a return to the world of Wodehouse.

In an article in Andersen Consulting's magazine *Outlook* (1999, Number 1), my ex colleagues Joel Friedman and Toni Langlinais suggest that:

Already taking shape are the first networks of product and service providers allied to satisfy the intentions of today's savvier, more sophisticated consumer. These alliances of providers, some of which have been formed through loose groupings around complementary products and services, are emerging examples of what we refer to as Intentions Value Networks.

Jeeves might be surprised to find himself described as an Intentions Value Network, but that is in effect what he was. He stood at the hub of a network of providers whom he directed to meet Bertie Wooster's intentions. He acted as filter and interpreter, shaping providers' products and services so that they best met the demands of his particular never-satisfied customer.

Many of the functions that it required a Jeeves to fulfil in the 1920s can now be carried out with the use of information technology. The Internet allows groups of specialised providers to come together into a network to meet consumers' intentions. And consumers can enter the network at any point. They can access individual providers directly; so they do not need a Jeeves as well as the providers themselves. Whichever provider they first contact acts as their integrator, their Jeeves, to enable them to satisfy that particular intention.

Firms will be highly motivated to work in this way— for Andersen Consulting's research suggests that within this new integrated business model providers will be able to increase their profit per customer significantly. The increase, however, will come from pooling data about customers, information which traditionally they would have zealously guarded, and from co-ordinating the providers' offerings.

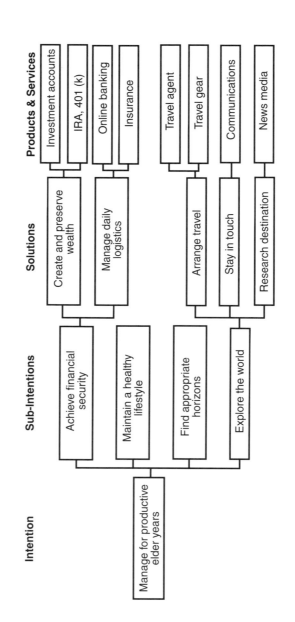

Figure 4.3   How the Networks Work

An example of how networks can work is the 'Manage for Productive Elder Years' intention (see Figure 4.3).

One example from Andersen's research involves an Intentions Value Network that is aimed at helping consumers move to new locations. Such a network already exists in embryo form in HomeAdvisor, a Web site launched by Microsoft in August 1998. HomeAdvisor combines products and services that help to satisfy the 'moving to a new community' intention. In order to fulfil the service on offer, Microsoft has already formed partnerships with American Finance & Investment, Principal Residential, RE/MAX, SchoolMatch and RentNet.

With such a network, Andersen Consulting estimates that a mortgage provider can expect to convert approximately 40% of referrals from the network's real-estate brokers into sales. That compares with the 25% average conversion rate for independent mortgage brokers in the United States.

There is an added benefit to this business model, however. Once a customer has used a network, all the partners learn more about that customer's needs and preferences. They can thus gain a better idea of how they can (together) deliver a customised package of goods and services that will in future fulfil that particular customer's intentions.

This virtuous circle was well described by Joel Friedman and Toni Langlinais in their article.

Continuous sensing and responding between the Integrator and the network partners drives a virtuous cycle of value between the network of customers and the network of providers,' they wrote. 'The more customers contribute insights and invest emotional equity in the community, the greater the insight provided to the partners, and the more they can make their products and services relevant to the needs of the customers. This strengthens loyalty and brand value. Existing customers have reason to return, and new ones are attracted; this, in turn, attracts and retains the best partners.

Members of a network have a distinct competitive advantage over firms that are not affiliated with others in this way because they can pool their customers and thus greatly reduce their acquisition costs. They can also pool their knowledge of customers and modify their product and service offerings accordingly.

In the world of intentions, customers and providers will have a fundamentally different relationship from the one they have today, or even from the one that the providers of solutions will have with their customers tomorrow. It is the difference between what Jeeves did for his customer, and the service that the local grocer provided in the same era when delivering, together with the groceries that had been ordered, some (unrequested) produce 'because it's just come in and I knew you'd like it'.

Providers will have to have an even deeper understanding of their customers' values, needs, behaviour and preferences if they are to satisfy their overall intentions. This is likely to lead to the development of value networks that specialise in satisfying the intentions of particular communities of buyers. Jeeves would have found it hard to work for anyone who was far removed from the English gentleman style of Bertie Wooster. He would not have understood the values and inclinations of, say, an early twentieth-century Pittsburgh steel baron. Likewise, the Intentions Value Networks of the future will seek to serve limited communities—pensioners, for example, or Generation Xers—because networks will tend to build up detailed knowledge and understanding of particular groups.

It will be very difficult for old-established firms to adapt to this new world of intentions. For a firm to meet a customer's intention it will have to truly understand what the customer is looking for, and be able to integrate the individual solutions of multiple third parties into precisely what the customer wants. Who do you know that is capable of doing this today?

5

Dimension Two—
The Customer as
Dictator

TODAY'S MARKETS ARE ESSENTIALLY SELLER-DRIVEN. IT IS the seller who decides what is produced and how it is sold. Customers, by and large, play second fiddle to the sellers and have to suffer the consequences of arcane organisational structures that do not act in a co-ordinated way when in dialogue with their customers.

But customers are changing. They are becoming increasingly demanding, aided and abetted by new technology. Sellers are no longer able to dictate terms in the way that they used to, and the organisation that does not take this powerful change on board is going to have a brief life in the twenty-first century.

Organisations are going to have to restructure themselves so that they become customer-centric, in other words, enter into a symbiotic relationship with their customers. And then they are going to have to adjust to the fact that markets might become buyer-driven, with customers specifying what they want and on what terms. Sellers are being pushed out of the driving seat.

Consumer power

By and large, corporate structures have not been designed with customers in mind. And this is becoming an increasing source of friction between consumers and businesses. Most companies today are built up of a number of separate divisions or functions, each of which has only limited co-ordination with all the others. So a customer of a bank, for example, can easily receive a new credit card just a few days before he or she receives an application form for the very same card. The organisation's left hand, in this case the marketing department, is too often not aware of what the right hand, the renewals department, is doing.

Customers' queries are frequently pushed from pillar to post within the same organisation. 'Yes, I can tell you your outstanding balance. But you'll have to talk to sales about our new mutual fund. I'll just pass you over. Oh, I'm sorry, they're engaged at the moment. Please hold the line.' And the customer is left listening to yet more supposedly soothing music that signally fails to fulfil its purpose.

Of course, in practice, customers are increasingly not left listening to the music. They hang up in anger and take their business elsewhere, because they have a growing number of options.

Developments in information technology are broadening consumers' choice and improving the information on which they base that choice. The Internet, for instance, is providing enormous amounts of information about products and prices, information that consumers simply did not have access to in the days before anyone was online.

And the current stage of development of the Internet is

positively primitive. There is much further to go, in directions that will ensure that the dissemination of information increases dramatically in both volume and scope.

Developments in broadband networks—the capacity to handle massive inflows of data, text and multimedia content—have been responsible for making Internet connectivity universal. For the future, wireless networking promises to take that connectivity one step further. Consumers will have access to vast quantities of online information right in the palm of their hand, wherever they may be.

And that information will give them enormous power. For example, they will be able to make extensive price comparisons on the spot. And that is sure to put a great number of producers also, in another sense, 'on the spot'.

The technology to enable this to happen is available even now. Nokia mobile telephones can already access Internet servers in order to obtain information on weather conditions, airline schedules and stock quotes. Combine that with the technology of the Personal Digital Assistant (PDA) and you have a mechanism for fundamentally shifting the balance of power between buyers and sellers.

Add in the fact that the prices of these gadgets are falling like autumn leaves, and the fundamental shift becomes a revolution. Everybody will be able to 'shop on the hop', rich and poor alike, ruthlessly switching from one seller to another as prices change or as their fancy takes them.

High-tech gizmos will no longer be playthings for playboys. Silicon chips will be embedded everywhere and even the ordinary man-in-the-street will soon be buying chickens with an implanted (and disposable) chip that will instruct his oven to turn itself off once his bird is cooked.

Consumers' new-found power is enabling them to be more demanding in all sorts of different industries. In the market for medicines, for instance, anybody can today find out about a host of complaints with just a few clicks of a computer mouse. They can then quiz doctors about their diagnoses and question their prescriptions. This begins to shift the location of the drug-purchasing decision—away from doctors and into the hands of patients.

In the banking business, customers are polarising into two groups: there are those who want an 'execution-only' service, for making transactions and shifting funds about. And there are those who want a high level of advice in order to meet their (relatively) complex financial needs.

The execution-only customers are looking for a commodity-type service based almost exclusively on price. And this is an area where traditional banks stand little chance of competing. There are always new entrants with lower costs who are prepared to undercut their prices. In the high-level service market too they are having difficulty competing. The needs of customers there tend to be too sophisticated for the 'high street' type of financial institution.

Empowered customers look set to turn the banking industry upside down. Not one of today's banking giants has anything like a guarantee that it will be in existence in 10 years' time, let alone still a giant.

The ability of information technology to arm consumers everywhere with vast quantities of information is increasing competition everywhere, as economic theory says it should, and in that way it is sharply reducing prices.

The availability of near-perfect information has led to the phenomenon of 'reverse markets'. Companies like priceline.com have led the way with auctions in which customers dictate the terms and conditions on which they are prepared to make a purchase, and suppliers then come forward if they are prepared to meet those terms. priceline.com is one of the first organisations to move into the buyer-driven section of the 'Cube' (see Figure 5.1).

One of priceline.com's services, for example, turns the tables on the traditional relationship between mortgage suppliers and homebuyers. Its Web site gives homebuyers the opportunity to tell a panel of lenders on what terms they will take out a loan. Any lenders who are interested are then able to put forward their best offers.

priceline.com happens to be an American company, but there is no reason why it could not put together bidders and vendors from completely different parts of the globe, someone seeking a mortgage on a property in Penang, say, with a mortgage provider from New York. Many more markets are thus set to become truly global—because the Internet knows no national boundaries.

One beneficial side effect of this for consumers will be that fewer industries will be able to benefit from cross-border anomalies. The enormous disparity in price between computer equipment bought in Europe and the same equipment bought in the United States will shrivel. And in the European car market, prices are sure to level off. The differentials that currently exist between the price of the same car bought in different countries will gradually disappear.

The problem for empowered consumers will soon become not one of a shortage of information but of an

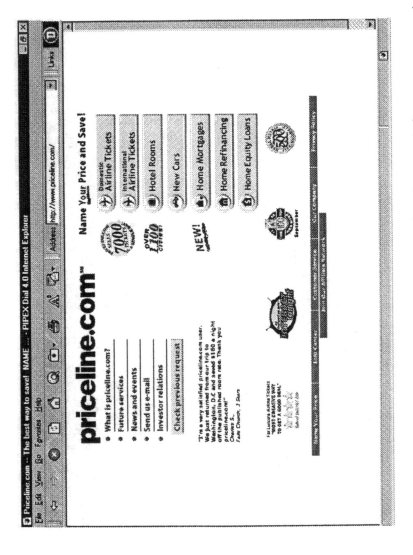

Figure 5.1   priceline.com is a forerunner in the buyer-driven market. *Source*: priceline.com at www.priceline.com

excess of it. 'Information overload' is already beginning to leave consumers baffled by so much choice. But rather than forcing them to revert to their old ways, this is merely creating a demand for firms to act as intermediaries, as go-betweens that can structure the surfeit of information in a way in which customers want to receive it.

Amazon.com was an early example of this new breed of commercial intermediary, what Forrester Research analyst Julio Gomes has called 'a content-focused matchmaker'. These firms, he says, 'help consumers make buying decisions when buying decisions are difficult.' Amazon provides this role by providing the opportunity for online reviews to be written and filtered. This allows Joe Public to make a selection from what otherwise may seem like identical products for his needs.

Amazon.com is not a publisher. It is an intermediary between the consumers of books and the sellers of books. It became an early trusted 'navigational guide' around the choppy waters of the Internet, and it was in large part because consumers quickly came to identify and trust such guides that eCommerce took off as quickly as it did.

According to the influential Yankee Group, an 'influx of well-known and trusted brand-name merchants to the Internet' was one of the most important reasons for the rapid rise of eCommerce at about that time. Among other things, a trusted online brand overcame buyers' fears about the security of online transactions.

Becoming customer-centric

These two powerful drivers (demanding customers and technological developments) are gradually pushing companies to become more customer-centric. 'Customer-centric' is a much-used term that means different things to different people. The way that I define it is to mean that every time there is an interaction between a customer and a supplier, both sides benefit from that interaction.

Many companies are conscious of the need to become more customer-centric. But they find it difficult to think about how they are going to transform themselves into an organisation that takes caring for its customers more seriously. How are they going to get from here to there? They have an existing culture and a structure that is built around product or channel 'silos'. In many cases they find that the fundamental transformation required in order to grow a customer-centric culture is too daunting.

Many firms are only making half-hearted attempts to become customer-centric. They integrate many unrelated databases that they have built up over the years, and then they add IT capabilities in the hope that this 'band aid' is going to give them superior knowledge of their customers.

In some cases, organisations have invested the money needed to develop electronic customer information systems that have the capacity to transform the organisation. But much of this money is often wasted because the customer knowledge is not disseminated adequately throughout the organisation.

A February 1999 survey by the UK's Chartered Institute of Bankers (CIB), carried out in conjunction with Andersen Consulting, found that only 6% of the bankers surveyed were confident that their institutions provided their staff with a broad view of customer data across all distribution channels.

Organisations are failing to take on board the change

of mind-set that is required at all levels—from the most senior managers down to the travelling salespeople working at the coalface. For sure, salespeople nowadays travel with their laptop computers and they keep in electronic contact with colleagues through Lotus Notes and other software. But they still tend to think that they're in the business of selling products, not of making sure that customers gain as much from their transactions as they do.

The human factor counts for a lot. People remain loyal to firms for years for quite irrational reasons. 'They were wonderful to my father', or 'I ate in this restaurant the day I asked your mother to marry me'. Reasons like that can over-ride the occasional slip in quality.

One business where the need for a totally integrated experience is particularly important is the airline business. A plane can take off exactly on time, and touch down precisely as and when indicated. But passengers will not be satisfied if they have, for example, had to wait around on the tarmac for ages before being able to disembark. Or if they have had a lousy meal—provided these days, almost invariably, by outside caterers that might not be under the airline's close control.

Many of the traditional flag-carriers have failed to take account of the fact that passengers blame the airline for their whole experience—the food, the baggage handling, the overcrowded runway, etc. Airlines can plead until they are blue in the face that airports are 'nothing to do with us', but that's not the way that passengers see it. They want a seamless flying experience, and they will travel with whoever can provide it.

And increasingly they have options. There was a time when the major routes were, at best, duopolies. But a number of newcomers have been able to make inroads into the business by pursuing niche strategies. Richard Branson's Virgin Atlantic, for instance, took advantage of the fact that the traditional transatlantic carriers had become over-concerned with filling seats in order to add revenue. Virgin focused on the business passenger, a high-paying customer segment that had become unhappy with being compelled to sit in a sardine tin full of backpackers. Virgin tried to improve the quality of the whole experience for its business-class customers, offering them extras like a limousine service to and from the airport at both ends of the flight.

When the whole experience is good, customers will come back for more . . . and more and more. The value that can come to an organisation from getting customers locked in for life can be enormous.

For a start, the cost of gaining a new customer greatly exceeds the cost of retaining an existing one. Mike Harris, chief executive of the Prudential insurance company's banking operation and the man responsible for the launch of its pioneering Egg service, reckons that the profits of a card company can be doubled if the company is able simply to extend the average period that it retains its customers from five years to seven years.

Market spaces

Customer-centric organisations have to forget about traditional markets and about their own 'share' of those markets. That is a concept based on products, on physical 'things'. It is possible for that sort of market share to be increasing to the satisfaction of the board, shareholders and senior managers at the same time as the market itself is about to be wiped out.

IBM, for example, became the world's largest company by being king of the mainframe market, a product-based market par excellence. When that market shrivelled to nothing (at a relatively slow rate by today's standards) IBM had a couple of extremely uncomfortable years while it learnt to adjust to having almost 100% of next to nothing.

Instead of thinking about markets and how to increase their share of them, customer-centric companies have to think about 'market spaces' and about how to dominate them. For market spaces last longer than markets. They include things like 'personal mobility' or 'financial security', needs that can be met by the products and services of several different markets. What would happen to the automobile market, for instance, if all our urban needs for personal mobility were met by buses and trains, not cars?

In notoriously fickle markets like toys, companies are on far surer ground if they think of themselves as filling a part of a market space called 'kid's playtime', not a market for objects called 'toys'. For a start, they will realise that their space is constantly being invaded by a host of new electronic alternatives.

Market spaces are not static, and companies need to keep an eye out for the ways in which they are changing. Subtle shifts, for instance, have occurred in the market space served by pharmaceutical companies. At first, pharmaceuticals were all about the management of disease. People didn't pop pills, by and large, unless they were ill. They had to have a disease before they became a potential customer for a pharmaceutical company's products.

Then the market space shifted and it became more like

something called 'managed health care'. Preventative medicines became as important as those that cured disease. In this market space, pharmaceutical firms did not have to wait until someone was sick to make a sale.

The next move may be to a market space called something like 'extended life and well-being'. Here pharmaceutical firms will produce medicines that serve customers throughout their lifetime, keeping them well during that time and giving them more time in which to purchase the firms' products. The more successful their products are then, the greater will be their customers' lifetime. And, *pari passu*, their lifetime value.

The pioneers

Many businesses have already recognised the need to focus more clearly on their customers. In a 1998 survey of senior executives carried out jointly by the Economist Intelligence Unit (EIU) and Andersen Consulting, customer demand was named as the number one force affecting business strategy. Moreover, the executives believed that it would become even more important in the future.

Half of the 200 leading companies in the study said that by 2002 their businesses will be segmented by customer. More than half said that they will be using eCommerce to transform their relationships with their customers, and 95% said that they will have data warehousing systems in place that will bring together and consolidate information on individual customers.

Despite the difficulty in translating intentions into actions, a few pioneering companies have begun to take steps towards becoming truly more customer-centric.

Among them are companies like Hewlett-Packard, Levi-Strauss, Xerox, Harley Davidson and Rosenbluth International, a large travel-services group. Manuel Diaz, a vice president at Hewlett Packard, told the authors of the EIU/Andersen Consulting report:

We know how to listen to the customer. We don't just invent something and find someone to use it. We invent useful things by listening to the customer first. That gives us a significant competitive advantage.

Harley-Davidson, the motorbike manufacturer, found an original way of listening to its customers. In the early 1980s it set up the Harley Owners Group (HOG), a forum where company employees regularly meet customers. At the same time, Harley decided to sponsor bike events where employees could mingle with customers and hear about their complaints and their wishes.

Hewlett-Packard (HP), the computer company that virtually invented Silicon Valley, is another good listener. It recently talked at length to a number of its large business customers, companies whose annual expenditure on computers and information technology ranged from $3 million to $1 billion, and it asked them what they wanted. The overwhelming conclusion from the company's enquiries was that its customers' most pressing problem with IT was 'the burden of managing overwhelmingly complex technology'.

Its customers wanted Hewlett-Packard (and any other IT supplier, for that matter) to give them not products but solutions—in the shape of better ways to manage and integrate their complicated systems. Products inevitably spelt problems. What customers wanted was someone to solve those problems. That applied whether they were in the business of manufacturing automobiles, selling mobile phones or of providing banking services.

As a result of its findings, Hewlett-Packard has divided its big customers into five different categories (see Figure 5.2). The categories are based on the value of the customers' purchases from the company, and on the complexity of their systems:

1. In the first category, called 'customer intimate', are HP's most valuable customers, high spenders with highly complex systems requirements.

2. The second category is called 'investment accounts', and in it are firms whose systems are still highly complex but who do not spend as much as firms in the first category. HP's aim is to move these customers up and into the first category.

3. In the third category lie the big spenders, firms who buy a lot from HP but whose systems are not particularly complex. The aim here is to make the relationship with these customers more valuable, either by moving firms up to a higher category or by increasing the efficiency of delivery.

4. HP calls the fourth category 'value-added reseller centric', and it includes firms which buy on a small scale but which have highly complex systems. These are often small, technologically adept firms that are unlikely ever to reach HP's higher categories.

5. Finally, the fifth group consists of customers with relatively uncomplicated systems and small orders. This group is called 'product support'.

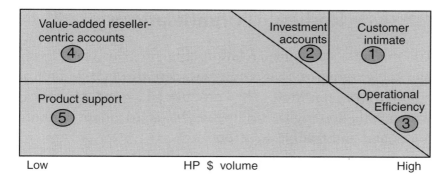

Figure 5.2   Hewlett Packard business categories

The segmentation enables HP to serve customers with different needs in ways that are valuable both to it and to the customer. But, as Mr Diaz says, 'Obviously we can't provide solutions profitably to all customers'.

Another company that decided early on to become more customer-centric was Levi-Strauss, the inventor of blue jeans. For Levi's the move involved making some painful decisions. In February 1999, Bob Haas, the great-great nephew of the company's founder, announced that Levi's was to shut down half its US plants with the loss of 5,900 jobs. The reason for the closure, he said, 'is to focus our energies on the consumer'. He went on to admit that the company's rip-roaring success between the mid-1980s and the mid-1990s may have dulled its sensitivity to its customers.

Customer retention is dependent on loyalty and loyalty is only created by truly understanding and meeting customers' needs consistently. Retention is the key to profitability. A satisfied customer is more likely to give an organisation more business; it is certainly less vulnerable to competitors' offers.

Radical reorganisations

To manage customer relationships in this new way inevitably requires that companies go through a radical internal reorganisation. The 'product silo' type of vertical structure is too rigid. Companies need to adapt a more horizontal and flexible structure.

Change needs to be focused on four different areas:

1. organising the company around new customer-driven divisions;
2. flattening the structure so that there is an increased emphasis on front-line staff;
3. developing multi-skilled teams with increased responsiveness; and
4. improving the links between front-line staff and the organisation's back-end processes and departments.

Kate Harmon of Andersen Consulting's Customer Relationship Management group has described this more horizontal type of structure as one which 'abandons the old economics and management theories based on hierarchy, bureaucracy, predictability and control. Rather it advances theories based on flexibility, adaptability, integration, and most importantly the production of customer satisfaction.'

When Harley-Davidson went through a process of restructuring in order to get rid of its old vertical organisation, it moved to a structure in which three circles of influence overlapped at the centre. The circles—called Create Demand Circle, Produce Products Circle and Support Circle—were designed to emphasise collaboration.

'We drew the organisation chart as three interlocking circles', the company's president Jeff Bleustein told *Fast Company* magazine in 1997, 'because there's so much interdependence among them'.

Reorganisations like this invariably arouse fears of job losses among the workforce. But Xerox, a much larger company than Harley-Davidson, went through a restructuring in the 1990s for similar reasons and it did not eliminate a single job during the process. Instead of cutting jobs, it redefined them. 'We're putting more people up front', said one manager at the time. 'The more they can make decisions, the less management you need'.

Xerox's reorganisation involved setting up a number of business teams that were tied to specific markets, and that were free to manage their time in a way that best suited the needs of their customers. A typical service team consisted of six technicians linked by pagers and two-way radios to a controller who was able to contact members of the team within minutes of a customer's call. In the states of Indiana and Kentucky, where the new structure was first rolled out, Xerox saw a 10% increase in sales in the first year, an 11% increase in employee satisfaction and an 8% increase in employment.

The travel-services group Rosenbluth International took an unconventional approach in its search for a more customer-centric structure. Rather than setting out to create something entirely new, it looked around for existing organisations that it felt could provide the level of customer satisfaction that it was aiming for. And its founder Hal Rosenbluth stumbled onto the structure of the typical American family farm.

Rosenbluth felt that on the typical American farm

everyone had to communicate with everyone else. (Obviously he had not read Jane Smiley's *One Thousand Acres!*) Moreover, as he saw it, everyone had to carry out specific functions and yet at the same time be knowledgeable about other people's functions. Those were the characteristics that he wanted for his company.

Since the whole company was too large to be treated like a single farm, Rosenbluth International was broken up into more than 100 separate business units, each with its own bunch of customers. The units were designed to behave like family farms, and fellow workers were encouraged to view each other as friends. The company's headquarters became the equivalent of a farm town where 'stores' (like human resources and accounting) could be purchased by the farmers.

Dramatic restructurings like those described above require the commitment of all the organisation's employees, from the very top to the very bottom. And that is not always easy to obtain—for a very particular reason.

A horizontal organisation requires a completely different management style from a vertical organisation, a style that is unfamiliar to most of the executives who are being expected to introduce it. During Xerox's restructuring, its chief executive confessed that 'the hardest stuff is the soft stuff—values, personal style, ways of interacting'.

There are aspects of any such restructuring that old-timers will inevitably find distasteful. For instance, they will be exposed to criticism from all directions (possibly for the first time in their lives). And they will have to adjust to the fact that decision making becomes something that has to be shared among a number of people. Most company structures are built on the idea that, at the end of the day, there is one (and only one) individual who is responsible for each decision. Abandoning the idea that, at some stage, 'the buck stops here' is not always easy.

A customer-centric organisation has to have an ambiguous power structure. Loose co-ordination between the company's executives is what integrates the different functions and comes up with products and services that meet customers' demands.

Training of executives to prepare them for this new culture is essential. Harley-Davidson provides its workers with 80 hours of training each year, training that focuses on specific competencies which the company believes that employees in a customer-centric organisation need to have. AEFA (American Express Financial Advisers) trains its top managers to build up teamwork within the organisation and to develop horizontal measurement systems.

But most firms have not done anything like as much. The EIU/Andersen Consulting study found that only 21% of the executives interviewed believed that their senior employees were well prepared to manage a customer-centric organisation in the year 2010. Firms are certainly starting to recognise the importance of customer-centricity as the Andersen Consulting survey demonstrated. Some of the key points of this are highlighted in Figure 5.3.

Customer-centric technology

Technology is making it easier for firms to become more customer-centric by enabling them to have a much deeper understanding of their customers' needs and of their buying patterns. But firms have to start not with the things that the

By 2002:

- 50% will organise by customer type (up from 18% today)
- 70% will revamp customer processes, with integrating sales and service top priority
- 53% will use electronic commerce to transform customer relationships
- 95% will have data warehouses consolidating information on individual customers
- 75% will provide differentiated customer treatment
- Retention of customers rather than acquisition will be the number one goal

Managing customer relationships
lessons from the leaders

Primary research with nearly 200 leading companies around the world, of which largest proportion was Financial Services

Figure 5.3   Estimates of the progress towards customer-centricity. *Source:* Anderson Consulting and the EIU.

new technology can do, but with the way in which that technology is purchased. Decisions within customer-centric organisations about investment in technology have to be taken in radically different ways.

In the traditional product-focused organisation, IT purchasing decisions were made in a way that was frequently not in the best interests of the company as a whole. Speed of performance was the main criterion. Computer-illiterate decision-makers in the product silos felt obliged to purchase anything that gave them an extra inch of speed, regardless of whether that was of any real value to the company as a whole or to its customers.

The customer-focused organisation seeks ideas from everybody in the organisation in order to formulate a technology strategy that concentrates on improving customer service. This strategy starts with the assumption that all new technology will not necessarily be of value to all companies. The customer-centric company understands that technology alone cannot create customer satisfaction (Figure 5.4).

The technology requirements of the customer-centric organisation will be concentrated on:

1. A **central master database** of all customer information, including a record of all contacts that have taken place between the organisation and each customer.

2. An **integrated multi-channel architecture** with a central repository of processes, content and interfaces that can deliver data to a variety of channels (call centres, the Internet and a mobile sales force, for example).

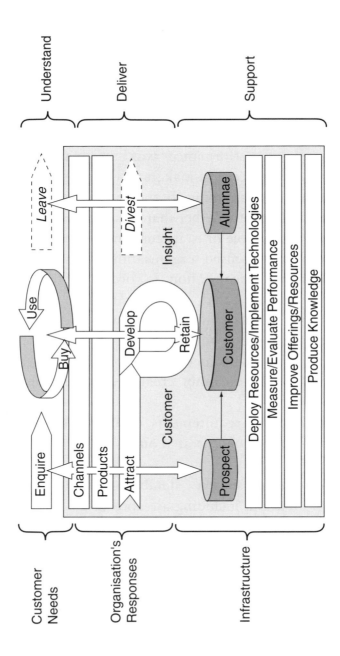

Figure 5.4   The marriage required for customer centricity

3. **Access channels,** each with unique end-user devices and network characteristics, but which share a common business logic.

Rosenbluth International has invested a great deal in advanced information technology that links every one of its 100-plus business 'farms' to minicomputers in Philadelphia. These computers are filled with client information that enable any Rosenbluth agent anywhere in the world to find out the travel details of any client who walks through their door.

A centralised electronic tracking centre monitors how many calls are coming into each farm, how long customers are waiting on hold, and how long each call lasts. This data provides the company with the raw material with which to improve its service even further.

The most revolutionary technology for companies and customers, however, is one that goes beyond giving help to customers who walk through the door. eCommerce via the Internet, brings purchasing options to customers before they come anywhere near a door.

For consumers, eCommerce holds out the promise of mass customisation—of having products tailored for specific individuals, but of doing it en masse, shifting to the mass market what had previously been the exclusive preserve of the wealthy, a bit like what Henry Ford did with the automobile.

Marc Hayes, from Andersen Consulting's eCommerce group, says:

Electronic commerce and the Internet may ultimately present the best channel for consistently delivering differentiated treatment of valued customers. The inherent ubiquity of the medium enables extended enterprises to bring complete knowledge of the customer—buying histories, psychographics, profitability, service histories, etc—to bear on each customer interaction. This customer knowledge, coupled with a company's business guidelines on how to offer differentiated customer treatment, can be used to better meet customer needs and build customer loyalty in a cost-effective manner.

As the Internet's role as a distribution channel grows, one challenge for organisations that want to be customer-centric is, 'How can we make purchasing on the Internet a warm sort of experience that consumers will want to repeat?' Most companies still need to understand more about what it is that persuades a consumer to switch to screen-based purchasing.

Initially, it was suggested that security was a major concern of consumers when making online purchases with credit cards. But that was undermined somewhat when people realised that consumers are perfectly happy to give out their card numbers to complete strangers over the telephone when buying 'direct'. The number of people prepared to disclose their credit card details online is growing rapidly.

Of much more importance is the design of the vendor's Web site. Consumers are clearly not equally enthusiastic about all of them. Some are (literally) more switched on than others. Companies that initially treated the Internet as a peripheral phenomenon which they did not need to take too seriously, have come to realise that they need to put considerable resources into making their Web sites 'visitor-friendly'.

Early sites were all about the raw presentation of information. Levi-Strauss's Internet manager Alisa Weiner described where her company went from there in the EIU/Andersen Consulting report:

With the Internet we're starting with information on where to buy. The next place for us is relationship marketing, developing programmes to ask consumers about preferences on products and communications . . . we want to know where they live, where they shop and how often they come in contact with our brand . . . it is very resource-intensive, and we've got a lot of technology right now, but until you actually apply it and put it in place, it's only a tool. The big revolution is changing people's mind-sets and helping them understand the role of relationship marketing in the overall mix.

That's a cry echoed by others.

Toyota's approach to its Web site was based on the idea of providing entertainment. As well as giving standard information about new models, industry statistics and the company's performance, the Japanese car manufacturer's site also features a guided tour of the Toyota classic car museum in Nagoya, together with news and information about motor racing. Initially, the scope for two-way communication between the company and visitors to its site was limited to simple e-mail messages, but it is the company's intention to build up the level of interactivity over time.

Amazon.com's founder Jeff Bezos gave the EIU/Andersen Consulting study some hints about Web design.

'Most Web sites,' he said, 'err on the side of having too

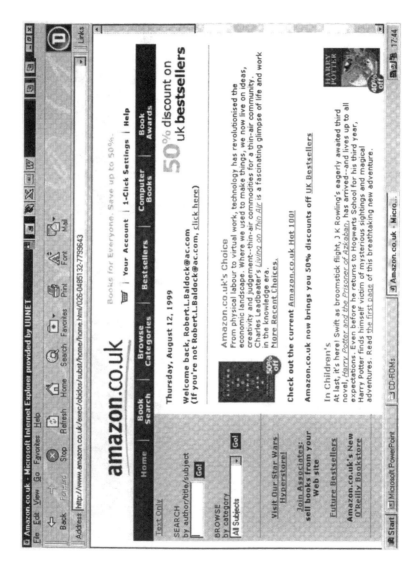

Figure 5.5   Amazon aim to bring personal touches to their Web site. (Reproduced by permission of Amazon.co.uk)

many graphics. I think that without slowing things down, we can have our Web site look as if it is designed to better convey our personality. The other thing we do is make everything on our Web site as obvious as possible. "Search" is highlighted. We try not to make it clever at the expense of obviousness'.

'If we have 4.5 million customers, we should have 4.5 million stores', Mr Bezos said in another context. This is illustrated by the way in which Web sites use cookies to recognise returning users. A cookie is information stored to the hard drive of a computer that contains information telling the Web site what hardware is being used and other possible data on the user. Amazon.com for example welcome you by name to their Web site through a personal greeting once an online transaction has occurred via your PC (Figure 5.5).

The Internet creates the possibility not only of creating personalised products but also of creating personalised electronic stores, a different one for each individual customer.

The early and successful 1-800-Flowers site emphasised the importance of making sure that the online shopping experience retains some of the 'offline' characteristics that customers are familiar with. Its Web site was designed to ape the way that people actually buy flowers in a real florist's shop—by price, by occasion and by the relationship between the buyer and the seller.

In 1998, Esther Dyson, a consultant and publisher described by the *New York Times* as 'one of the most influential figures in all the computer world', told *Outlook*, Andersen Consulting's in-house magazine, that companies need to understand that the Net gives consumers 'more control, more power'. 'To succeed in business there', she said, 'you need a certain lightness of foot, even a sense of humour . . . but most of all, you need to have good, creative people, not just technologies or systems'.

'Even more so on the Web than in the real world', she continued, 'you build your brand equity by doing something of value for people, not simply by advertising something of value. And there's a crucial difference there. Amazon.com would not be doing so well against the online challenge from Barnes & Noble were it not for the fact that Web users have such a positive and productive experience when they actually visit Amazon's site.'

Amazon's Jeff Bezos also emphasises the value of brands and points to some of the competitive advantages that this gives to the old-timers. Their real advantage, he says, 'is brand-name familiarity, and brand names are more important on the Internet than they are in the physical world. On the Web, there are no external cues, or at least there are fewer. With Amazon.com's Web site, for example, you can tell there's a lot of work going into it. But it's not the same as seeing a 40,000 square-foot bookstore. Brand name becomes incredibly important online'.

But Esther Dyson thinks that in this Web-based customer-centric world 'the big guys are not necessarily going to be the winners . . . The usual advantages of economies of scale, for example, are far less a factor in the online world. Look at Amazon's Associates Program, which gives hundreds of independent sites a share of any Amazon books they recommend and sell at their sites. I think that's a very clever strategy by Amazon. What it's really doing is renting out economies of scale to small players. So superior resources or economies of scale by themselves are not enough to win online'. That's a clear warning and a challenge to the large corporations of yesterday.

The buyer-driven world

Beyond the customer-centric world lies the 'buyer-driven world', a world that we are only just beginning to glimpse. It is a place where technology is able to perform feats that we can still scarcely imagine, a world where the consumer is not so much a king, more a 'dictator'.

In this world, all consumers will carry with them, all the time, small portable devices no bigger than an old-fashioned cigarette case. These will be a development of sophisticated mobile phones that are already on the market, and they will become global accessories, found in handbags and briefcases all over the world.

They will incorporate GPS and broadband communications all in one, and they will provide consumers with all sorts of electronic services wherever they are. In this world, all business will be transacted wherever the customer happens to be—on top of a mountain or in the middle of a forest. Figure 5.6 describes some of the traits of the buyer-driven business environment in relation to our cube Framework.

One of the electronic services provided by these devices will be something like an experiment called Shopper's Eye that was conceived at Andersen Consulting's Center for Strategic Technology Research (CSTaR) in Palo Alto in the 1990s. Shopper's Eye enables producers to send to consumers (at any time and to any place) competing electronic offers that meet needs which they guess (from the consumer's personal profiles) that they might have at that moment.

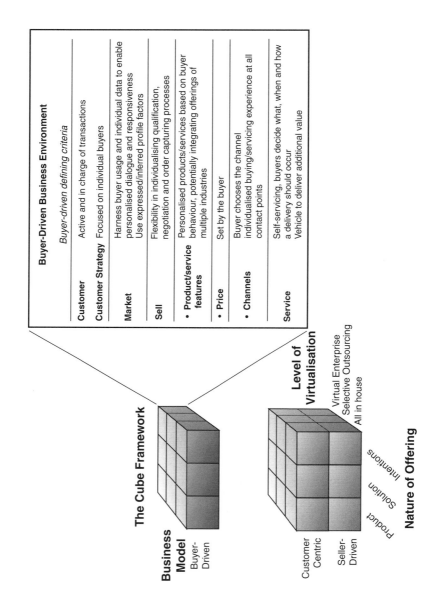

Figure 5.6 The buyer-driven business environment

The first 'page' of the Shopper's Eye opens with a map of the area around the consumer. On it are recorded the location of prominent stores and, marked with a cross, is the consumer's current position. But just as the (potential) buyer knows where the sellers are, so the sellers know where the potential buyers are. So these neighbouring stores compete electronically, via the Shopper's Eye, to tempt the passers-by inside.

Another part of the device's electronic service will be akin to something called BargainFinder—an intelligent agent, also developed by Andersen Consulting. BargainFinder started life as a simple program for searching the Web in order to find the lowest prices for music CDs. But it (and programs like it) will be expanded in the future into high-volume, fee-based intermediaries that match buyers of commodity products with a group of aligned providers. It will become a tool for busy people to search the Web for whatever item they want.

People who don't want to do the searching themselves will be able to use one of the many agents who will spring up to act as intermediaries between buyers' demands and the wealth of information and choice thrown out by sellers.

Agents will put consumers' demands out into the marketplace and will field all the responses, purchasing the one that gives their client the best value for money, and informing them electronically of what has been done.

The Shopper's Eye service might open with a screen showing the consumer where he or she is at that moment. Subsequent screens will show which vendors have been persuaded by the consumer's profile (of their earnings and past shopping habits) to try and entice them into their stores.

One screen might show in full moving colour a number

of special offers carefully targeted at the consumer's lifestyle. For instance, Harrods, the department store, might have a new line in organic dog food that it is keen for dog-owners to be aware of. It will be able to show dog-owning consumers a little video of a canine that looks just like theirs eating the new organic biscuits with relish.

On the next page Thomas Cook, the travel agent, might be offering special tours based on its knowledge of airline tickets that the consumer has already purchased elsewhere.

Consumers wanting to make a purchase 'on the hoof' will have to give the machine the answers to a couple of questions (like, do they want the goods delivered or will they collect them?) and the number of their credit card. To do this, they won't even have to make any keystrokes because by then voice recognition systems will enable the device to transmit the consumer's spoken message electronically to an agent and, through the agent, to the relevant producer.

These agents are going to be powerful intermediaries whom consumers trust enough to leave them to find the best offers that meet their particular needs. So, for example, whenever consumers make a list of groceries and household goods that they want to buy, they will mail it (and the price that they are prepared to pay) electronically to their agent who will put it out into the marketplace. Big supermarkets will then respond to the agent with their offers for that particular bundle of goods.

The marketplace will be so competitive that consumers will find that they are buying from Tesco one week, from Sainsbury another, and from Safeway a third week. For purchases such as these there will be little loyalty to a single vendor. Purchasing decisions will be based almost solely on price, as with any commodity. Loyalty will lie with the intermediary service agents who will have to actively promote their name and brand image as being trustworthy.

Another service that consumers can come to expect from these electronic devices is constant monitoring of their health. Someone, for example, walking briskly across an open stretch of park might suddenly hear his watch give out a shrill high-pitched bleep. The back of the watch will be able to monitor various aspects of its wearer's condition. So if his blood pressure rises sharply, for example, the bleeping will be a reminder to take a pill and a rest.

It will also alert medical professionals to the existence of a potential customer. For the sound will be picked up by the Shopper's Eye device and transmitted to hospitals and doctors in the area. They will not only receive the alert electronically, they will also receive full details of the potential patient and his or her medical history.

Another capability of the Shopper's Eye device will be to keep an eye on the consumer's home. Developments of something called 'Magic Home', a service that also began life in Andersen Consulting's Center for Strategic Technology Research, will tell consumers what's left in, for example, their food cupboards and their refrigerators. This it will do via sensors that will have become standard in food packaging and that will connect with other sensors set into everyone's domestic appliances. The Magic Home service will be able to order automatically from a service provider any items that are missing.

This may sound slightly fantastical and far away. But don't be fooled. A number of successful companies are already planning for a future along these lines.

6

Dimension Three—
Stop Doing Everything

FOR MUCH OF THE TWENTIETH CENTURY, COMPANIES believed that the way to be in control of their destiny was to own the means of reaching that destiny. They owned their own plant and equipment; they owned their own employees—in the sense that all their employees worked full time for them, and for them alone. They often owned their main suppliers and their main distributors too. Or, if they didn't, then they frequently thought that they ought to.

Vertical integration, the idea that it is advantageous to own organisations that are immediately upstream and downstream from your own operation, was immensely popular in the second half of the twentieth century. Firms in the oil industry, for instance, spent great energy vying to see how much further up or downstream they could go than their rivals. The likes of BP and Shell owned everything from the oil in the ground to the drills, the tankers, the filling stations, and the factories that turned the stuff into petrochemicals. That sort of vertical integration, by definition, gave birth to ever-bigger giant corporations.

Gradually, however, a bunch of pioneering firms showed that ownership was not all that it was cracked up to be; that it carried great costs and that it was dangerously inflexible. They showed that there was another way.

Their view was that the individual firm should concentrate only on its core competencies, on those things that it did particularly well and at which it had a competitive advantage. A main implication of focusing on core competencies, of course, is that anything that is not a core competence should be handed over to someone else.

Many of the pioneering firms were the early franchise operators—fast-food outlets like McDonald's and Kentucky Fried Chicken, for example. The franchisees laid down tight rules on production and service. Their core competencies were the processes involved in this production. But they then left people who were not employees of their firm to get on with the rest of it. And in many cases these people helped the companies to put in extraordinary levels of performance.

Another early much-written-about role model was Benetton, the Italian fashion firm. It relied on a large number of small outworkers scattered around northern Italy to produce its goods, and on a large number of small franchisees all over the world to sell them. To the traditional vertically integrated firm this diffusion of operations seemed dangerously anarchic.

But they were unable to ignore the company's success. Customers loved Benetton's shops and products, and the profits rolled in. Others sought to emulate the Benetton formula, in which the company itself remained narrowly focused on only a small number of the processes that were required to change raw materials into garments.

Benetton bought the yarn and it controlled the design of the garments. It was also in charge of the dyeing of the yarn (in a high-tech just-in-time process that became world famous), and of the marketing (where, again, the firm's billboard advertising became world famous).

Whatever it chose to put its hand to, it did in an expert, if unconventional fashion. At some stage, the company had decided what it was good at, and it had then focused on those things—its core competencies—and only on those things.

This model—of selectively 'outsourcing', handing over to a third party, processes that had for years been considered to be an integral part of any firm—was developed further in the 1990s. The case for it was made more compelling by the failure of a number of large conglomerates (like ITT and Hanson Trust) to continue adding value to the bunches of disparate businesses that they had almost randomly gathered together over the previous decade.

At first, outsourcing seems to involve shrinking the organisation, and that is something that many chief executives find hard to contemplate. For some, it's even tougher to accept that there is anything in their organisation that can be done better by others. But that breed is dying. The more difficult hurdle to surmount is to put aside the idea that their organisation is, in effect, going to be 'downsized'.

In many cases this downsizing is a redistribution of assets, not a writing off. Under the terms of most outsourcing contracts, the staff, plant and equipment that are carrying out the tasks in-house are transferred lock, stock and barrel to the outsourcing firm. The same people do the job, but as part of an organisation of fellow experts that respects and develops their special skills.

Nowadays no company can afford to ignore the opportunity that selective outsourcing gives to improve performance and return to shareholders. But for many, this should be only the first step along a road that leads them before long to become a virtual organisation, an organisation that outsources almost everything, retaining for itself only one or two core competencies, things at which it is truly excellent.

For this is the corporate structure of the future, the only one that will allow organisations to be sufficiently flexible to meet the demands of those ever-more demanding consumers that we heard about in the previous chapter.

There are a small number of firms that have already established themselves as virtual organisations, firms like the Virgin group in the UK, which is largely a marketing operation but which markets everything from train tickets to pensions, and a company called Monorail Computers in the United States. Monorail outsources the manufacture of its computers as well as the ordering, the delivery and the accounts receivable. Only the design is handled in-house.

Companies like these share a number of common characteristics:

1. they rely heavily on technology to keep costs down;
2. they focus narrowly on their core competencies;
3. they build up their brands; and
4. they leave everything else to reliable behind-the-scenes third parties.

The great advantage of virtual organisations is that they are able to move very quickly in order to seize new market opportunities. And that is going to be a vital skill in the twenty-first century. They form alliances with whoever and whatever is needed in order to meet consumers' demands as and when they arise. And sometimes they change partners in mid-stream as the business develops.

Such firms are able to run rings round their old-established competitors. They start with a different cost base and they can switch strategic direction overnight. They are leaving the giants standing.

Outsourcing

Outsourcing is not an entirely novel concept. There have always been certain functions which have, for the most part, been outsourced to others. One of the most obvious is advertising.

Most companies leave the production and origination of their advertising campaigns to 'advertising agencies'—i.e. they outsource it to third parties. This was the norm even before an American naval officer by the name of Commodore J. Walter Thompson got into the business in the 1880s.

Likewise, companies have been able to outsource financial functions such as factoring and leasing, the outsourcing of the accounts receivable function and of capital funding, for many years.

It was only when companies tried to come to grips with the fast-changing world of information technology in the 1980s, however, that the benefits of more widespread outsourcing became evident.

For as long as IT was centred on a mainframe in the basement of corporate headquarters, companies could justify managing it all by themselves. But the introduction of the mini-computer diffused IT responsibility out to corporate divisions. Each of them was asked to make their own decisions about equipment and the management of it. The introduction of the PC thereafter had the effect of diffusing this decision making even further—right out to managers who quite literally did not have a clue about computers, or about something that was becoming even more important—the interface between computing and telecommunications.

For a while, expensive mistakes were made. But when a few firms had demonstrated that handing the management and development of IT over to a third party made both financial and operational sense, a bandwagon started to roll. Most firms were swiftly reassured that outsourcing did not deprive them of some essential part of their being. The extraordinary growth of firms like EDS and CSC in the early 1990s demonstrates how willing companies are to take the plunge.

Once the idea of outsourcing has been accepted for IT, it is easy to see how it makes sense in other areas, particularly areas with a high level of specialisation, such as logistics. The VolvoGM Heavy Truck company in the United States, for example, has outsourced all the stocking and distribution of its spare parts to FedEx Logistics Services. This arm of Federal Express runs a toll-free line and a warehouse in Memphis stocked with VolvoGM truck parts.

Procter & Gamble, the consumer-products manu-facturer, manages an inventory of disposable nappies on behalf of Wal-Mart, the big American retailer. In both cases, the level of service provided is far superior to that which the buyers of the service were able to provide for themselves.

The idea of outsourcing has now spread to areas like marketing and finance. The London Stock Exchange, for example, has handed over the running and development of its price-information systems to Andersen Consulting. From an 'all in-house' philosophy, even organisations as sensitive to the need for confidentiality and tight control over their business as the London Stock Exchange have moved to a 'selectively in-house' philosophy.

The growth of outsourcing has not, in itself, struck a blow against corporate gigantism. One of the reasons why companies left their IT to others was because those 'others' could reap economies of scale from the massive amounts of processing and systems development that they were able to undertake. The firms to which work was being outsourced were often giants themselves.

Their size was boosted by the staff and assets that were handed over as part of the outsourcing contract. In most cases these employees saw the move as advantageous. They were invariably going from a company where they were a 'side-show' to one where they were the main event. It was like a theatre company where the set designers have had to suffer years of corporate indifference while the director and the actors got the lion's share of the budgets and the applause. Suddenly the set designers found themselves working for a company which did nothing but build and design sets. There, at last, they had equal call on the budgets, and on the plaudits.

There is another powerful argument in favour of outsourcing besides the fact that it allows one organisation to reap economies of scale while another firm shares the benefit. That is that it allows companies to stay ahead of the latest developments in whatever area it is that is being outsourced, something that they cannot hope to do on their own.

The latest hardware and the latest means of networking are thus at every manager's fingertips, however computer illiterate he or she may be. For outsourcers bring highly specialised knowledge and skills to bear on the activity—as well as economies of scale.

The difficulty with outsourcing lies in the long-term nature of the commitment involved. The typical outsourcing contract can last for up to a decade to allow the outsourcer to recover the costs of any up-front investment they have to make in the function(s) that have been outsourced to them. Even when companies are happy to hand over the running of their IT operations to acknowledged experts, they want to share fairly in the (invariably unpredictable) gains from outsourcing for the whole duration of the contract.

The only way they can do that, since no corporate crystal ball is clear enough to see so far ahead, is through some sort of partnership arrangement. So outsourcers increasingly seek to develop contracts in which both parties in some way share the benefits (whatever they might be) over the whole period of the contract. And as they share the rewards, so they also have to share the risks. This inevitably brings the two parties much closer to each other, and much closer to understanding each other's needs and problems.

These long-term outsourcing relationships have become a significant feature of the business world, joining the much wider corporate movement towards strategic alliances—partnerships between two or more organisations in which both share the risks and the rewards of the activity being carried out by the partnership.

The future is alliances

The formation of alliances was one of the dominant forms of corporate activity in the 1990s. This phenomenon did not receive anything like as much media attention as the many mergers and acquisitions that were taking place at the same time, but it played an equal part in determining the corporate structure that will prevail in the twenty-first century.

By the end of the 1990s, alliances were estimated to account for over 20% of the revenues of the top 1,000 American corporations, double the figure at the beginning of the decade. By 1997, alliances were being formed at such a rate that the average American bank that year had three times as many alliances as it had had a year earlier.

No one is too big. In fact, the bigger the corporation, the more likely it is to form alliances. IBM set up over a thousand different strategic alliances in the 1990s, while AT&T, General Motors and General Electric have set up many hundreds. And these have not just been with smaller firms that they can dominate. The big firms also form alliances with each other. AT&T, for example, has an alliance with Microsoft to provide broadband services via cable-television networks.

Even if, as many claim, a large chunk of these alliances are no more than glorified supplier contracts, there have been enough deals where both parties have put in equity— where, as one Shell executive described it, 'each parent puts in a rib'—for the trend to have considerable momentum.

There are several forces driving these alliances. A number, for example, follow the logic of the outsourcing alliance, where both parties want to share in the risks and the rewards of an activity in which they both wish to participate.

The oil company Chevron, for instance, formed an alliance at the beginning of 1998 with a number of companies that it would normally have used as straightforward subcontractors. It joined with Aker Maritime, Brown & Root, Han-Padron Associates and Saipem to provide a full range of deep-water drilling services—from conceptual studies and engineering to fabrication and heavy lifting. All the companies in the alliance agreed to share the risks and the rewards of the alliance's high-risk activity—looking for new oil and gas reserves in the Gulf of Mexico.

Another common reason for forming an alliance is to get a toe into a foreign market. Consultants Booz-Allen & Hamilton estimate that more than 20,000 alliances were formed world-wide between 1996 and 1998, and that approximately 75% of them were across borders. This helps to explain why alliances are more common in Europe and Asia (where there are lots of borders) than in the United States. Europe and Asia account for half the world's total; the United States for a third.

In some industries, alliances are useful for getting round problems specific to that industry. There are hundreds of alliances in the airline industry, for example, because national carriers are restricted in their ability to own foreign airlines. In many cases, the only way they can go global is through alliances. Maybe British Airways would have chosen to merge with American Airlines given half the chance. Instead, the two have formed a complex alliance that involves several of their operations.

Another sound reason for forming alliances is to get at

the brain power that big companies find it increasingly difficult to attract. In many industries, the most talented young people today want to work for small organisations. They prefer to work for small biotech start-ups, for instance, than for the large pharmaceuticals firms that were the previous generation's preferred employers.

This is partly to do with money. The small start-ups are able to offer talented people a relatively more attractive package. A typical deal would include equity options and a high level of responsibility at an early age, perks that are more difficult to enjoy in large companies.

As a result, the big pharmaceuticals firms now devote up to 20% of their research budgets to joint ventures with young biotech firms. The number of biotech alliances formed by the top 20 pharmaceutical firms more than doubled during the 1990s.

Despite the proliferation of alliances, however, it is not (and never has been) easy to make them work. People who have been involved with alliances vow that they are more difficult to manage than mergers. But they can be a lot more rewarding.

Forming an alliance is often said to be a bit like getting married, and like marriage it requires the partners to take a leap of faith. Peter Boot, the man in charge of alliances at Corning, an American chemicals company that is often cited as being particularly good at managing its alliances, agrees that much depends on trust. He told *The Economist*:

> You have to be disposed towards the most benign interpretation of the strange signals that you get from time to time. You have to interpret them innocently.

Relying on trust, however, has a particularly attractive side effect. As Philip Sadler points out in his book, *Designing Organisations: The Foundation for excellence, 3rd ed*, (Kogan Page, 1988), 'Trust is on the whole cheaper than controls'. Leaving someone to get on with the job— motivated almost only by the desire to work with you again—is very much less costly than setting up complicated internal controls to make sure that everyone in-house does what is expected of them.

To continue with my marriage simile, alliances can also end up in divorce and in the courts. Unlike mergers and acquisitions, which are virtually impossible to untangle and, therefore, once consummated continue almost indefinitely, alliances are by their very nature destined to be temporary.

In the early days it was common to find practitioners arguing that, in good alliances, the contracts were filed away at the beginning never to be referred to again. But this was a hangover from thinking about more-or-less eternal mergers and acquisitions. Alliances are not eternal: the average one lasts less than five years, and most undergo a major restructuring within three.

Alliances were also often thought of as a first step along the road to merger. Executives at Lotus Development, for instance, maintain that their company's alliance with IBM ultimately led to the offer from IBM to buy the company. There is plenty of evidence, however, that alliances can actually discourage acquisitions. The downstream joint venture between British Petroleum and Mobil, for example, never led to the full-scale combination of operations that its creation had led many to expect.

The brief and finite nature of most alliances is not

necessarily negative, however. Some alliances are formed only for the purposes of a specific project, and then disbanded when the project is finished. For instance, 10 of the world's biggest drug firms, including Glaxo Wellcome and SmithKline Beecham, have set up a joint research project to study variations in human DNA. The project has a predetermined and finite life.

This sort of temporary venture is the fastest growing type of alliance—the alliance that is formed to achieve interim objectives or to hedge bets. Other such ventures include Delta Air Lines now defunct code-sharing agreement with Virgin Atlantic. The venture, aimed at gaining Delta access to London's Heathrow airport, lasted for three years. National Westminster and Tesco's co-branded debit card lasted nine months.

Some alliances inevitably end in failure. Andersen Consulting reckons that some 30% of them fail altogether, and that another 23% achieve only limited objectives. The reasons for failure vary from cases where the expected value of a deal clearly does not materialise, to cases where the deal's champion moves on to pastures new.

The most common cause of failure, however, comes from a failure to appreciate that alliances require a completely different style of management thinking to mergers and acquisitions. In particular, they require managers to think about their exit routes at an early stage.

A few firms do think long and hard about exits before going into alliances. They include complex terms in their contracts that resemble those in a pre-nuptial arrangement.

But many firms still don't, influenced perhaps by the feeling that it is somehow disloyal to look for the way out when still on the way in. Despite the constant warnings of lawyers, an Andersen Consulting survey in 1998 found that only 65% of alliances had specific exit clauses. This is foolish. As one of my ex colleagues has put it:

Today, executives are behaving like Napoleon—either assuming that no exit will be needed or that the Russian winter need not be calculated into the battle plan.

Ice-cream maker Ben & Jerry, for instance, had a sticky time unwinding its alliance with Dreyer's Grand Ice Cream, its well-connected distributor for almost a dozen years. Ben & Jerry decided to end the alliance when Dreyer's put in a cheeky (and unwelcome) take-over bid for the ice-cream firm.

But Dreyer already had control of over 70% of Ben & Jerry's distribution. So taken aback was the ice-cream maker by what it saw as Dreyer's disloyalty that it was eventually pushed into a distribution agreement with arch-rival Hagen-Dazs.

The need to take due care of exit routes is being heightened by the changing nature of alliances themselves. In the early 1990s they were set up in a narrow and unambitious way. Chemical companies went into manufacturing joint ventures, and little else; banks joined international clearing arrangements like Visa and Swift; and consumer-product companies like Procter & Gamble enthusiastically embraced alliances for market-entry strategies. But they all shunned any sort of deal that did not involve equity.

Since the mid-1990s, however, alliances have become much less permanent and much more fluid. A common pattern is for two firms to come together and agree at first to co-operate in a fairly narrow area. They then either continue to co-operate in this narrow area—and ultimately bring the deal to a close—or they move on to a broader area of co-operation. From there they either fall back again or carry on to a full merger or acquisition. Almost all alliances today are in this sort of flux, a state in which they are changing and evolving almost continuously.

Beyond alliances

Alliances today are mainly about enabling companies to escape from the constraints of their current market space and, at the same time, to move into entirely new market spaces. Take the example of the Scottish banks.

For well over a century, banking in England and Scotland was a separate affair. The London clearing banks handled the business in England and Wales and the Scottish clearing banks had the market to themselves north of Gretna Green. Both groups agreed not to encroach on the territory of the other, although the Scottish banks were allowed to have a branch or two in London.

But then in the 1980s the chill wind of competition began to blow and the Scottish banks found themselves unable to break free from their small domestic base. They did not have the financial resources to buy into the English market or to build up de novo branches there. Their future looked at best uncertain.

Until, that is, the nature of the competition in their industry was turned upside down by technology and deregulation, and they suddenly found things working in their favour. When non-bank institutions in England—organisations like the supermarket chains Tesco and

Sainsbury—decided to enter the banking business, they (and the UK regulator) wanted them to begin in alliance with an experienced partner.

Tesco briefly went into partnership with NatWest, one of the biggest English banks, but NatWest soon found the link with such a direct rival uncomfortable. Before long, the Scottish banks had become the partner of choice of anyone from outside financial services who wanted to enter the English market. Not only are they not English (and not competing in that market), but they also have a long-standing reputation for tight cost controls and excellence in financial services (insurance and fund management as well as straight commercial banking).

The Scottish bank's new partnerships in England demonstrate a fundamental feature of the alliance phenomenon—they are partnerships of specialists who come together in order to compete in a new market or to compete more strongly in an old one. Tesco offers its powerful brand name to a new banking service, but behind the labels on the automated teller machines stands an anonymous Scottish bank and its excellent systems.

Once a firm has entered into such a relationship and understood its potential value, it reaches a crucial stage where it has to ask itself what it is that it should actually be doing. In all these new business relationships, what is it that it has to bring to the party?

The virtual enterprise

The answer to that question may end up being: 'Very little'. In the United States, for instance, Larry Sundram decided that he wanted to set up an insurance company, but he started with a deep desire to employ very few people. In the event, it turned out to be remarkably easy to satisfy that desire. InsureDirect subsequently renamed to Reliance Direct pays Xerox to print all its documents, an advertising agency to do all its marketing and promotion, and a call centre to handle sales, claims and queries. Larry sits 'virtually' alone in his office holding all the bits together.

Reliance Direct is one example of the virtual organisation. There are many others. The UK's Virgin is perhaps the most famous. In the mid-1990s, the Virgin organisation captured about 5% of the UK cola market with just five employees. It achieved this by an extraordinarily tight focus on a single specialism—marketing. Everything other than marketing, including the actual production of the drink itself, was done by someone else.

Virtual organisations can now be found in almost every industry. The Italian motorcycle manufacturer Aprilia, for example, does not make a single component of the bikes that carry its name, despite the fact that it is one of the most famous marques in the world. *Business Week* described Aprilia's offices as looking 'more like a California software house than a motorbike manufacturer'. Everything is bought in from a network of suppliers spread across northern Italy, a pattern reminiscent of the pioneering structure of Benetton.

More than anything else, the virtual organisation fosters a different mind-set. It starts by questioning everything that the firm continues to do for itself. It begins with the assumption that it can get rid of everything, and only then starts to think about which elements of the business are so critical that it has to keep them in-house.

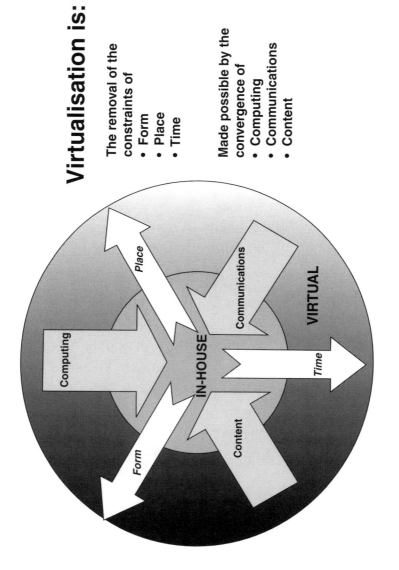

Figure 6.1   Virtualisation defined

My definition of the process of 'virtualisation' (See Figure 6.1), something that a growing number of companies are going through, is that it is:

The removal of constraints of form, place and time made possible by the convergence of computing, communications and content.

This is not something that occurs overnight. Virtualisation is currently taking place gradually every single day in many different firms. As the business environment changes, and as more emphasis is placed on the need for speed and flexibility, firms are finding the advantages of virtualisation more and more compelling

Removing constraints on form

Developments in video-conferencing and global mobile telecommunications are radically expanding the possibilities of corporate structure, dragging it away from the monolithic vertically integrated giant that was the most sought-after option of the twentieth century. The most sought-after form for the twenty-first century is likely to be a more amorphous organisation, consisting of a small centre around which swirls a fluid, multi-faceted set of alliances. This is very much like the swarms of fish that formed and reformed in the series of pioneering television advertisements that Andersen Consulting ran in the mid-1990s.

One example of this form of organisation identified by my colleagues at Andersen Consulting is what they have called the global network. This is a multi-partner alliance with operations on three or more continents which Andersen's Peter Fuchs says is, from certain vantage points:

One of the most alluring new forms of organisation, capable of providing unparalleled purchasing scale, momentum for new technology platforms and seamless global product or service delivery.

Examples of such networks include the Visa credit card organisation and the Coca-Cola bottling network. These have been hugely successful in creating value, yet they are not in themselves large organisations.

Some global networks have failed to live up to their promise. In 1993, Cable & Wireless set up a 48-member federation of telecoms firms that spanned the globe. But it was abandoned three years later—in part because it fossilised itself by immediately setting up a complex three-tier committee structure. On some of these committees all 48-member organisations had to be represented. By not building in the flexibility and informality that is essential if these new forms of alliance are to work, the venture was doomed from the start.

The formation of one of these global networks is almost always preceded by a number of less ambitious alliances. For example, Germany's Lufthansa airline already had a marketing alliance with United Airlines before the two launched their ambitious multi-partner Star Alliance. And the global alliance between British Airways, American Airlines and Quantas is built on a number of regional alliances that have been forged quite separately by each of the big three partners. British Airways has a Euro-centric link with Belgian, French and Irish airlines, while American has links with Chilean and Canadian regional flyers.

These regional links do not threaten the central global link since British Airways, for instance, has little interest in fostering US–Chile routes. And likewise Quantas has no wish to be a competitor with anyone within Europe. Not for the moment, anyway. What the airlines' customers get out of the alliance is a seamless, hassle-free way of booking tickets anywhere on their combined networks.

Many of the most eye-catching global networks have been formed between giant organisations—a 'one per continent' sort of thing, in the way of the airlines. But the global network is a structure that suits smaller firms as well. Many professional service firms have adopted it, often as an amalgam of partnerships rather than of corporations. Colliers International is a network of real-estate agents around the world, for instance, and BDO International is a loose-knit network of accounting firms from over 80 different countries.

Moreover, many of the larger international professional service firms act as if they were a network of smaller firms, even when technically they are not. The firms' offices in faraway places—in Moscow or Buenos Aires, for instance, are given a great deal of autonomy. There is some pooling of central services and of information, but each office is run much as if it were an independent business, entirely in charge of obtaining and servicing its own clients, and almost wholly responsible for its own profit and loss account. Clients benefit by getting a locally tailored service that is backed up by global weight and expertise.

That may go a long way towards explaining why the three most attractive employers to graduates in Europe in

1999 were consulting firms ,structured in such a way—namely, Andersen Consulting, McKinseys and the Boston Consulting Group. These networked firms genuinely provide the appeal of being both local and small, and global and large. The graduate in Germany joining one of them works inside Germany with German firms, but he or she has the opportunity also to set that local experience in a global context (via the firm's network) and subsequently to work almost anywhere they wish.

At the heart of the new organisational form is a switch from control to trust. Controls cemented together the twentieth-century business units; trust will have to be the cement of the twenty-first-century business units. An organisation built on outsourcing and networks of formal and informal alliances cannot thrive on old-style control, the sort that was perhaps most famously demonstrated by the Ford Motor Company after the Second World War.

At that time Henry Ford II introduced a rigid system that led one commentator to declare that, of the three organisations that he had worked for, the US Navy, the Jesuits and Ford, 'the Ford Motor Company was the most authoritarian, the most regimented, and the most driven by fear'. The company's notorious 'blue book' defined the jobs and the limits of authority for every single employee.

In general, control can be exercised within organisations in one of two ways—either through control of the detailed activities carried out by the firm's individual employees, or through control of the output of those employees.

In his book *Designing Organisations*, Philip Sadler defines the distinction as being that between Marks and Spencer—where the duties of a store manager are laid down in great detail and leave little scope for discretion—and the way in which an English pub is run. In pubs, the publican is allowed to run the business in a highly individualistic way (most English pubs are owned by a big brewery) for as long as there are enough satisfied customers to keep the tills ringing and the budgets met.

The way in which control is exercised has always been powerfully influenced by the technology of the day. Before the days of the telegraph, a company's units located abroad had to have a large degree of autonomy.

With the arrival of the telegraph, telex and international telephone, however, it became much easier for organisations' head offices to keep control over the outer reaches of their empires. The structures which they set up to do this were often modelled on the military, not surprisingly since most of the people running these organisations had had military experience of one kind or another.

One of their favourite models was of Winston Churchill running the Second World War from an underground bunker where hordes of assistants pushed counters across maps of Europe. Many companies came to be run a bit like that.

But the conflict in the Persian Gulf in the early 1990s awoke the world to the fact that technology had completely changed the rules of warfare. America's IT-intensive weaponry was devastating. Cohorts of ground troops working under an old-fashioned command and control structure did not stand much of a chance, however well organised they were.

With a brief time lag, much the same things have happened in the business world. Companies that work with structures built on old technologies are finding themselves in danger of being obliterated by competitors that are rapidly embracing the new technologies.

Removing constraints on place

Examples of the way in which technology is removing the constraints of place can be seen in the virtual office. The move from the industrial age to the electronic age is diminishing the primacy of physical assets. Work is less physical and tangible, more intellectual and portable. The actual spot where it takes place is of far less significance than it used to be when most people were expected to work from nine to five at more or less the same place.

Lester Thurow, a former dean of MIT's Sloan School of Management, gave a vivid description of the virtual office in his 1997 book *Rethinking the Future*:

Modern technology gives us new ways of organising a business. Just look at the office building. At the moment, if you walk into most office buildings in the world at, say, 10.35 in the morning, you'll find that 25–30% of the chairs are empty. The people who are supposed to sit in them are away doing something else—they are selling; they are at office meetings; wherever they are, they're not in their chairs. With modern technology you don't have to have all of that idle space and those unused computers and telephones. Instead, you could run an office building like a hotel.

You walk in and there's an electronic board that says room 1021 is empty. You go to 1021. You have your own personal telephone number. You call up your computer code. You press a button and your family picture is up on the flat-screen TV set on the wall. And that's your office for as long as you're there. The minute you leave, it ceases to be your office. We know why we don't do that at the moment: human beings like to have a cave.

But the first company that figures out how to make this work will save 25% on office space, 25% on telephones, 25% on computers. These will be the low-cost producers, and low-cost producers will inherit the earth.

A number of firms are heading in this direction, designing flexible workspaces to be used by employees as and when they require. Some of Andersen Consulting's offices, for example, have been reorganised along these lines. These 'virtual' offices not only help to reduce costs, they also help to speed up response times.

By eliminating its unneeded office space in a similar way, AT&T reckons that it freed up some $550 million in cash flow between 1991 and 1998. Other benefits included a more productive workforce. And the company reckons that it was better able to hang on to its star employees, people who tend to gravitate towards the aggressive new business entrants in search of greater flexibility in their pattern and place of work.

A worker's office is increasingly wherever their mobile phone and their laptop happen to be located. That can be on a factory assembly line or in the back of a taxi. Most commonly, though, it is in their home. As many as 40 million people in the United States now work from home.

Rather than, as in the past, being afraid that such workers would be too far outside their control, companies are finding that home-based telecommuters can be more productive than office-based workers. In one study of what was considered to be a well-managed office, it was found that distractions from work took up, on average, 70 minutes of every eight-hour working day. People at home, it seems, are distracted far less. Contrary to the general impression, they are not permanently zapping between different television channels or chatting with the neighbours.

This does, however, demand that companies find new ways for employees to communicate with each other and to form bonds that cement them to the same organisation. In an article entitled 'The Alternative Workplace' (*Harvard Business Review*, May/June 1998), Mahlon Apgar wrote: 'Managers and employees have to learn how to be in and of the organisation while not being at it'. This is a challenge that corporations will have to tackle in the early years of the next century.

And there will be no escaping it. For technology is about to increase dramatically the scope that people have to be flexible about where they work. A big technological leap is about to extend Internet access to mobile telephony, and this will further enlarge the opportunities for people to conduct business wherever and whenever they want.

Motorola, a leading mobile phone manufacturer, has reckoned that at the end of 1998 the world had 800 million fixed-line telephone subscribers, 200 million wireless phone owners and about 200 million users of the Internet. By 2005 it reckons that those numbers will have risen to one billion for all three: one billion fixed-line phone subscribers, one billion wireless phone owners and one billion Internet users. The fast growth and convergence of these different markets will be a key platform for future business growth.

A number of big companies in the mobile telephone and the Internet markets have already come together for the purpose of developing the two technologies. Motorola and

Cisco, the market leader in Internet networking equipment, have formed an alliance in order to develop Internet services on cellular networks. They have pledged to invest up to $1 billion in building up the infrastructure for a 'wireless' Internet. British Telecom and Microsoft have also formed an alliance to develop Internet and corporate data services on mobile devices.

What has happened with information technology in the wired world is to be followed by similar developments in the 'wireless' world. email and Internet access from hand-held 'smart' devices will permit people to order their groceries from the top of a bus in the same way that they now gossip with their friends from the top of a bus.

The 'day traders', those retail investors in the United States who play the stockmarket via online brokers, will be able to do their online dealing from their cars on their way to work, from their hotel rooms at the end of a day's work or, for that matter, from a tent in Antarctica. That will shatter any attempts to contain stock trading within prescribed hours and will, in all probability, make markets themselves much more volatile.

The convergence of mobile telephony and Internet technology is not, however, mainly about removing constraints on shopping, be it for stocks or for stockings. It is about changing the way in which business is transacted, about enabling people to work from the tops of mountains, or to design a new mass-market car (for example) via some sort of 'smart' hand-held device at the same time as they are trekking in the Himalayas.

Thomas W. Malone, professor and Robert J. Laubacher, research associate, at the Sloan School of Management at MIT, have given these 'remote' workers of the future a name. They have called them 'e-lancers', an elision of 'electronic freelancers'. An article by the two appeared in the Sept/Oct 1998 issue of the *Harvard Business Review*. Called, 'The dawn of the e-lance economy', it was ominously subtitled: 'Are big companies becoming obsolete?'

The authors' tentative answer was, 'Maybe'. They envisage a world in which business is not controlled by managers in large permanent corporations. Rather, it is carried out autonomously by independent contractors who are connected to each other by means of PCs and electronic networks. The fundamental unit of the new e-lance economy, they say, 'is not the corporation, but the individual'. The technology frees workers from the straitjacket of the large organisation, a straitjacket which fewer and fewer of them are prepared to wear.

Even innovation—or at least the modern form of it: IT systems design or process improvement—is being done in an e-lance way, in some cases removing the need for huge R&D departments. The Linux operating system, for instance, was invented by a 20-something Finnish undergraduate who posted his blueprints on the Internet and gave everybody free access to them. In return, he got all sorts of creative input and precious improvements—all for free. Now Linux is being incorporated into computers manufactured by firms as big as IBM and Dell. It stands to become the only serious rival to Microsoft's dominant Windows operating system.

Malone and Laubacher insist that the e-lance economy is not some sort of fantasy of the future. In many ways it is already upon us—in the shape of outsourcing and of telecommuting, and in the increasing importance within corporations of ad-hoc teams that are put together for the purpose of completing specific tasks, and that are then disbanded when those tasks are done.

Moreover, the authors say that the building blocks for the next stage of development of the business organisation for the electronic era are either in place or under development. They include, 'efficient networks, data interchange standards, groupware, electronic currency and venture capital micromarkets'.

This, they add, leaves a big question mark over the future of today's big corporations, the ones that have grown under a command-and-control style of management. Malone and Laubacher claim that 'today's small companies enjoy many of the benefits of the big without sacrificing the leanness, flexibility and creativity of the small . . . Whilst big companies control ever larger flows of cash, they are exerting less and less direct control over actual business activity. They are, you might say, growing hollow'. The authors quote the examples of ABB and BP which have 'broken themselves up into scores of independent units that transact business with one another almost as if they were separate companies'.

One consequence that the authors foresee is a return to medieval-style 'workers' guilds'. The large corporation of the twentieth century provided its employees with a number of 'welfare functions' that workers will have to seek elsewhere in the e-lance economy. Pensions are perhaps the most obvious example; but there are other support services—professional training, sickness benefits, union representation, etc.—that they may come to seek from new types of organisation which become much like the old craftsmen's guilds.

A number of such guilds still exist in places like the

City of London—the Honourable Company of Master
Mariners, the Merchant Taylors' Company and the Guild of
Architectural Ironmongers among others, their names
reflecting the professions that were powerful during their
day. A new breed of workers' guilds might perhaps include
the Honourable Company of Master e-Lancers or the Guild
of Merchant Outsourcers.

Removing constraints on time

If employees of the virtual organisation are being freed to
work more or less where they like, they are also being freed
to work more or less when they like. This is demonstrated
by the increasing number of part-time workers that are
being employed by big companies. These are no longer
found solely among the traditional low-status jobs that
have in the past been considered suitable for part-time
work—cleaners, receptionists, etc. Increasingly they are
highly paid professional workers, particularly women with
young children.

A study by McGill University in Canada found that the
performance of a sample of such professional workers was
considered as good as, if not better than when those people
were full-time workers. There was evidence that part-time
work increased the 'loyalty, motivation and commitment' of
the workers.

However, the McGill study found one of the big
drawbacks of part-time work was the failure to create
systems within organisations whereby star workers could
progress and meet their career expectations within a part-
time framework. Top managers still do not accept that the
most senior management jobs can be done in any way other

than full time, and with most of that time being spent 'on the spot'.

Even in innovative open-minded companies, the study says, 'there appears to be no real re-evaluation of the traditional career path to the top'. Such a re-evaluation is essential if companies are to continue to have access to the best talent in the virtual business world of the future.

7

The Journeys Ahead

WHEN YOU NEED TO TRANSFORM YOUR ORGANISATION TO respond to a seismic shift in the nature of commerce, what do you put at the top of your to-do list? That's a tough question, but it's one I set out to answer in this chapter.

Let's go right back to where we started. What does the future hold for Simon Jones, the big-company executive that we met at the beginning of this book? Basking in the self-satisfied glow of a successfully managed Y2K transition, his holiday plans were rudely interrupted by alarming news of a fast-growing competitor in Belgium. An Internet-based up-start had the temerity to grab market share that he and his legion predecessors had spent decades building. It was *their* market share. Secure ground that *they owned* and no one had dared attack them for years. Yet here it was, happening right in front of their eyes.

Previous chapters have explained that why this blip on the corporate radar spells big trouble. Not only will our unfortunate executive will have to put his holiday plans on ice and work out how to break the news to his family, but it's clear now that he could also have far worse news to tell them soon. Unless he thinks fast he could be out of a job. For a senior member of a monolithic organisation, the Internet can bear bitter fruit. Simon has just had his first taste, but it will not be his last.

Every time a loss-making Internet-based company joins NASDAQ (or any other exchange) on a stratospheric valuation, every time a share option sale creates a new Internet billionaire, we should spare a thought for our friend and the hundred others like him as they wonder what happened.

But let's not paint too bleak a picture. So far I have talked a lot about companies that are successfully taking their first steps into the future. It is true that many of them are start-up companies that seem to appear overnight. But nobody has a monopoly on smart ideas and innovation. Big companies too are working out what business models will fit tomorrow's future and are trying them on for size. As I will explain in this chapter, that is a strategy that makes a lot of sense.

As Richard Owen, the vice president of Dell Computer Corporation responsible for the company's Internet sales operation, said recently:

> *We're an $18.2 billion business trying to become an $18.2 billion-plus Net company. That's a very different business model from Amazon and Yahoo!*

When you face a barrage of new competitors, it is easy to feel shell-shocked. Everyone seems more innovative than you. You have a great line of products, but they are offering solutions. You think you know what customers want, but they let their buyers dictate terms. You have a world-class manufacturing and distribution capability, but they outsource everything.

It is true that new entrants can leapfrog established players. For one, they are not slowed down by baggage from the past. But that must not lead to paralysis. Firms that are to thrive in future must have leaders who can see through the maelstrom of change that will swirl around them in the years ahead and find a clear path into the future.

Finding a path

The Cube is not designed to be a map with each cubelet a separate stepping stone. The dimensions of the cube are not locked to a fixed scale. It is a schematic outline, like that of the London Underground—no more than a framework in which to think about the future and the major changes that are going to affect all existing businesses in general, and big ones in particular.

There are many ways to move from the point where a company does everything in-house and sells commodity-type products to the point where it is a virtual enterprise driven to produce whatever meets the demands of consumers. And every individual firm has to work out its own path, its own speed and its own destination.

The key point is that the current position of many leading companies is untenable in the long term—organisations need to change. But as I will explain later, it is a mistake to regard that final cubelet at the top right-hand corner of the back of the Cube as an ultimate destination. Not every company will want or need to travel that far. My experience of working with large organisations tells me that, by and large, a firm's journey through this three-dimensional space will involve break down into three distinct stages, stages that I call —Triage, Integrate and Buyerise.

Companies will have to move into these stages boldly. The sort of creeping incrementalism practised by many of them ('let's do something at the margin and see if it takes off') is worse than doing nothing at all. For it enables firms to fool themselves that they are doing something—in eCommerce or in bundling solutions, or whatever. But small somethings are going to count for nothing in the business world of the twenty-first century.

Three steps to heaven

Before I explain these three stages of the journey, let me just remind you of the nature and scale of the challenge that today's giants face. I firmly believe that the general direction of any company set on success in the twenty-first century is upward and onward through the Cube, from the bottom left-hand corner at the front towards the top right-hand corner at the back.

Most organisations need to achieve a substantial transformation across a number of areas if they are to reposition themselves for success in the buyer-driven world that we are all careering towards. Change is needed across customer, product and channel strategies and in the overall business and technology architecture for sales and service delivery.

Key elements of the transformation challenge include:

FROM	TO
Passive customers	Active customers
Supplier has the power	Consumer has the power
Product	Intentions
Standalone operations/channels	Buyer-driven channels
Vertical integrtation (in-house)	Virtual integration (shell company)

Given the wide gap between the way that most of our giant firms operate today and what they will have to do in a buyer-driven world, a strategy of phased transformation is the best option for most incumbents.

The Cube shows us that there are three axes that an institution needs to move along. The first two axes relate to the nature of demand. Firms need to evolve from offering standalone products that deliver focused value in traditional ways to solution bundles that bring together two or more traditional products to create tailored solutions, convenience and economies of scope. They then need to go further still to offer clusters of products and services that cross industry categories in order to meet underlying customer needs, what I call 'intentions'. I explained this in more detail in Chapter 4.

In addition, firms have to evolve their marketing approach. They need to move away from operating standalone channels tied to a narrow product range and not linked to other customer access points. In the future they will need to work with integrated channels that link together different customer access points *and* products to provide a seamless customer-oriented experience. Ultimately they will need to adopt (or compete against) true buyer-driven approaches that provide a personalised buyer experience and put the buyer in control.

The third dimension of the Cube relates to the supply side. Here, the sales and service delivery infrastructure needs to be part of a broader business design. Firms will shift from trying to do everything in-house around a vertically integrated business, and they will start to outsource functions that are not among their core competencies. Ultimately, firms will combine outsourcing with a range of strategic alliances to the point that they become true virtual enterprises.

Some of our threatened giants have already started their journey through the Cube. I explained in Chapter 5 how supermarkets such as Tesco are trying to package a number of products and services together in order to make life easier for their customers. They stack their shelves so that the pasta sauces are next to the pasta and the Parmesan cheese. The more innovative ones provide complete dinner menus with maps explaining where in the store the necessary ingredients can be found.

Some of these companies are seeking to provide solutions for customers rather than simple products. They are trying to help consumers to solve problems, like 'How can I entertain 16 eight-year-olds to tea today?' instead of simply enabling them to buy a series of products independently—party hats, balloons and cakes—and create their own solution.

The massive growth of sales in semi-frozen pre-prepared meals in western supermarkets in recent years has shown how eager customers can be to buy solutions. The UK has been the one with the highest per head capita consumption, a figure that has been growing at 28.4% a year in volume terms. France is currently arguably the most interesting market at the moment with high growth rates and a per head capita consumption that leaves plenty of room for growth.

I talked back in Chapter 4 about Zenda, the experimental service launched by the UK's National Westminster bank. With the aim of taking the hassle out of customers' daily lives, Zenda's telephone-based helpers try to answer all sorts of queries. Rather bizarrely, with this service has seen one of the UK's most traditional banks start helping its customer find places to rent storm trooper costumes for their Star Wars parties.

This experimentation is all well and good, but that is all it is—experimentation. In every industry I can think of, there is a massive gap between what the incumbents are trying to achieve and what the new market entrants are doing from day one. While our giant organisations experiment at the periphery, the companies that could well put them out of business are parachuting right into the heart of the future.

These new firms are *at least* customer-centric and outsourced. Some are even buyer-driven and making intention plays. While some of our more innovative giants are trying out different ways of outsourcing, empowering the buyer or meeting intentions, these new firms have it ingrained in their business plans, and in their corporate culture, from day one.

How do you make up ground and catch up with these new firms? One possibility is to throw resources at the problem—access to capital was always the traditional advantage of the big firm. You could try to make a big leap forward all in one go, but is that really possible with your creaking legacy systems, unwanted warehouses or unnecessary branch networks? Probably not. And if you thought you could, would you bet your business on it?

That's why I see the transformation journey as having three distinct stages. The first I call *Triage*, the stage in which companies need to be clearer about the profitability and value of their various customer segments and to sort out their customers according to their quality. In the second stage, which I call *Integrate*, firms need to become much more

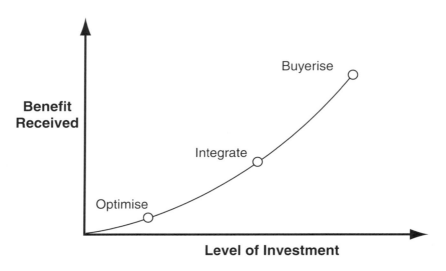

Figure 7.1   Three steps to Heaven

customer-centric. They need to think about matching their offerings more closely with their customers' needs. In the third stage, which I call *Buyerise* (See Figure 7.1), companies have to turn their business models upside down in order to survive in what will have become a buyer-driven world.

A company that successfully negotiates these stages stands a fighting chance in the battle against new market entrants. Some firms will find some elements of the changes that I am about to describe more difficult than others, but each is vital— none can be skipped. And firms need to take their first steps now. Not tomorrow or next Monday, but today.

Let's look at each of these stages in more detail.

Triage

Triage—The first step to excellence. Rationalise your basic sales and delivery economics to maximise customer profitability.

Before you set out on any journey, you have to decide what you want to take with you. What is valuable and what can be left behind. That decision is the essence of Triage—the process of sorting according to quality, organising by degree of urgency. The Triage stage of the journey is about refocusing the organisation and preparing for the next step—identifying quality, maximising value and dumping any excess baggage.

Firms at this stage are not ready to start offering the innovative buyer-driven solutions that they will have to create if they are to thrive in the future. For now, the focus is on reducing costs so that when the firm moves forward, it can build on solid foundations rather than on sand.

To achieve this refocusing, you need to be able to understand your customers in a new way. You need to have an insight into their *full* potential and use that to identify ways in which you can sell them more. The aim is to stop offering the same products across the same channels to all your customers. Rather, firms going through Triage need to try and group customers into segments. They should then offer products that are tailored to that segment. Importantly, they should offer those products via the most suitable channel for that segment.

But even at this very first step in the journey, some organisations find it difficult to move forward. In the Triage stage, firms have to take a fresh look at their ongoing operations and start to analyse and understand profit in terms of customers, channels and products. Some will find this a major challenge. Every business should know already whether a particular product or channel is profitable. But many struggle to extend that analysis to different *mixes* of channel, product and customer.

In the banking business we know that a transaction carried out via the telephone costs half as much as the same transaction conducted over the counter in a traditional branch; and that an ATM transaction costs a quarter as much. But what about profits? To work out whether it is more profitable to sell to a particular customer segment over the phone, via the Internet or in person is more difficult. This requires a complicated process of allocating overheads and analysing data that a lot of companies just cannot handle. But it is not impossible—Spanish banks, such as Bank Inter, for example, are excellent at this.

Other firms are going to have to learn or buy this capability. The challenge in Triage is to act decisively to exit segments that do not make a profit and to move aggressively to reduce channel costs. But, as we shall see, that does not necessarily mean dumping whole swathes of existing and potential customers. Rather, it means finding more effective ways of doing business with them. The result is to remove gross mismatches between the potential value of a customer and the cost of acquiring and serving that customer.

Which are my profitable customers?

In the Triage stage the key strategic decision is which segments to exit and which ones to fix. It's a familiar adage that in most businesses 80% of the profits come from 20% of the customers. In my experience there are plenty of firms that are trading on far scarier percentages. As I explained back in Chapter 2, there are some banks that rely on 20% of their customers to generate 100% of their profit.

And it's not just banks that are exposed in this way.

Many big supermarkets also stay in business thanks to the 10% of customers who provide 50% of their profit. So a key goal has to be protecting that golden minority of customers that keeps the firm in business. If they stop coming back for more, everything else is academic—the business will go down the tubes anyway.

These firms should be worrying about the prospect of a new entrant coming along and stealing their profitable customers. Unfortunately the truth of the matter is that they do not know sufficiently well which of their customers are profitable and which are not, or even why. They sorely need to analyse their costs more carefully and use this data to segment their customer base more precisely. Only once they have achieved that can they begin to nurture their profitable customers.

Even so, that still leaves the unprofitable majority— what of them? It is worth noting here that many organisations need to take a more enlightened view of customer worth. It's too easy to take a decision about whether or not someone is likely to be a profitable customer based on a crude snap-shot of their current circumstances. Wouldn't it be better to assess customers in terms of their likely future profitability, what I call their lifetime value?

It is possible to calculate lifetime value quite easily. You simply need to combine the information that you should be collecting already about people you do business with and the data you can buy about people to calculate what you can reasonably expect to sell them in the years ahead. An overdrawn, 25-year-old male, living in rented accommodation looks like a bad bet for financial services—unless he also happens to be a student doctor. Of course, students have always been cut a lot of slack on the basis that, when they finally get jobs, they will make good money and never move their bank accounts. But as people lead increasingly flexible lives and fewer people have traditionally recognised 'jobs', understanding of lifetime value needs to become more sophisticated and more widely used.

Having said that, there will still be customers who don't look profitable now and don't look much like becoming so in future, even on the most enlightened appraisal of their potential worth. What should you do about them?

The first option is to cut the cost of servicing low value customers. New technologies make it increasingly easy to separate premium customers from those that are less valuable and provide different levels of service.

The second option is to try to increase revenue from the unprofitable customers by selling them more services. One way of doing this is to simplify the firm's products so that they become cheaper and more affordable for these lower end customers. How many people use all the functions on their VCR, for example? Traditionally, competition fuels an endless drive to adorn products with 'benefits' and 'features' that often seem increasingly irrelevant. By offering simple, pared down products, firms can capture new markets. In South Africa, for example, Standard Bank launched a range of very basic low cost financial services products and reached a new audience of customers who had previously seemed hopelessly unprofitable.

Of course, if neither of these work there is always a third option—get rid of the customers who are never going to be profitable. This is a radical option that will, for some businesses, go against the grain of everything they do.

But it has to be considered. There are already plenty of professional firms, for example, that deliberately set out to shed 20% of their clients every year.

Rationalisation

A reappraisal of customer value (and the possibility that you may divest yourself of some of them) is just one aspect of the rationalisation that takes place in the Triage stage. Firms need to re-engineer their sales functions to lower the cost of both acquiring customers and of servicing them. The sales force can be rationalised and automated to reduce the time spent on non-productive activities—this can often allow downsizing of the sales force or greater customer coverage.

Other channels such as call centres can be consolidated and modernised to take advantage of scale efficiencies. Stores, branches and other outlets can be resized or relocated to maximise geographic coverage while minimising costs.

In the Triage stage, customers are often pushed into self-service channels primarily as a cost-saving mechanism. In the banking sector, for example, cash-dispensing ATMs and self-service kiosks are a substitute for branch-based staff. Initially such channels may actually increase costs because customers often use the new channel while continuing to use the higher-cost existing channels. To resolve that, firms will have to think about ways of encouraging customers to use the channels that cost the business less and discouraging them from using those that cost it more. In the UK, the Prudential's online financial services operation EGG offers premium interest rates to banking customers who only access their accounts via the Internet. But if those customers decide to call EGG's telephone banking line, they are charged.

In Triage, the business model will still be fundamentally seller-driven. The focus is still on reducing costs by simplifying products and channels, not increasing revenue. But when the firm has rationalised in this way and abandoned unprofitable segments, it's time to move forward.

Integrate

In the second stage of my recommended route through the Cube, firms take their pared-down products and distribution channels and their better understanding of customers, and they begin to build. Organisations move to a more customer-centric business model where their channels and products are integrated and closely aligned with the key buyer values of their customer segments, which will now be well defined.

They integrate channels and information to provide seamless service across channels. The more innovative ones will move slightly towards strengthening their hand through selective outsourcing. Finally, firms take their improved knowledge of customer segments and the needs of those segments to offer solutions, rather than products.

As I explained back in Chapter 4, I define a solution as a set of related products combined at the point of sale to meet a customer need. The closer firms can get to meeting the underlying needs of a customer (e.g. for a home) rather than selling the products which provide the means to achieving the need (such as a mortgage), the greater opportunity they will have to differentiate their offerings from those of competitors.

To date, an over-concentration on product has lead to a poor appreciation of the customer's real need—why do people want the product in the first place? I'm sure most marketing departments would balk at that idea and could hold forth at length on why people buy what their business sells. But what hard information would that answer be based on, and how accurate would it be?

Banks, for example, are notoriously bad at under-standing people's needs. In 23 years as a well-paid consumer of financial services, no bank has ever asked me what I really wanted! They have sent me questionnaires for sure. But only so that they can try and slot me into some broad consumer category or other. (Who's not A or B these days?) The banks' aim is not to try harder to meet the individual needs of me, Robert Baldock.

Perhaps that is too much to expect. But firms that have reached this stage of the journey should at least be able to slot me into a small and clearly defined segment of similar customers. They can then offer carefully tailored solutions to these chosen segments. If they don't know what I want, they can't do that and they will fail.

Of course, firms need to ensure that they make the most attractive offering to their most profitable customer segments. I often see examples of firms providing the fastest service to their worst customers. The ubiquitous 'five items or fewer' line at the supermarket checkout is a case in point. Re-organising your store so that some customers get a super-fast checkout is a great idea, but why then restrict that premium service to the people who probably do the least business with you?

All these firms have done is give their best service to their worst customers. Instead of five items or fewer, why not have a fast check-out for people with fifty 50 items or more? Or to people who come at least once a week? In the Integrate stage, firms need to think outside the box, bend the rules, and look afresh at how things are done.

This is an approach that some car manufacturers have adopted already. Nowadays, most of the successful ones use the same basic platform to produce a whole range of different cars. In most cases, the consumer is generally more interested in issues like how the car looks, who gets an airbag and whether there is air conditioning, not what is under the body. For example, a number of Ford and Jaguar cars share common components.

Some car manufacturers have gone a step further, however, and have started to allow individual customers to specify exactly what features they do want. BMW, for instance, now boasts that there are hardly any two of its cars on the roads today that are truly identical. And models like the The Smart car, a joint venture between the Swatch watch company and Mercedes-Benz, is turned out almost like a fashion accessory with an amazingly wide variety of colours and interior designs, which can be changed at any time simply by popping into the nearest approved dealer. This kind of innovation is taking these firms close to the next step of the journey, where the buyer dictates the terms.

Dell Computer Corporation is another example of a firm that allows customers to configure the product exactly how they want. Visitors to its Web site can start with a basic laptop or desktop model and then add or remove features so that they can buy a PC with the exact specification they want. And as they decide whether to go for a CD-ROM drive or DVD, for example, they can see the impact their choices will have on the price of the computer. Dell has recognised that different customers value different features, and is letting them choose which ones they want, rather than trying to guess in advance what their customers will want.

In the Integrate stage, firms not only understand their customers' needs, they also recognise that those needs change over time. So firms that have successfully segmented their customers and worked out their lifetime value (an ability acquired in the Triage stage) can now start to be more proactive.

With better information about customers, firms can anticipate changes in need and target those customers with appropriate offerings. If a customer has children, for example, when will they start school, when will they start wanting to use the Internet, when will the household need two PCs, will they need a loan to finance that and does that make the family more interested in online banking? Being able to target customers in this way also increases the chances of cross-selling them other products enormously.

When firms start to make offerings based on lifetime value and a continuous understanding of customer need, they can remove a lot of pointless product anomalies. Car insurance, for example, is typically sold as an annual policy. As a result insurers (for all intents and purposes) invite all their customers to look for a better deal from a competitor every 12 months. Why organise a business that way? Of course insurers will want to periodically reassess a customer's risk profile, but why do that every year? Most people will want car insurance for their whole lives (or at least until they are too old to be driving). So why not offer that—a car insurance policy for life? Insurers that I have spoken to find this a difficult concept. The annual policy review is at the heart of their business. Again, in the Integrate stage of the journey, innovative firms will think again about these basic product principles.

General Motors, for example, now sells cars with on board two-way telemetry. These smart cars can work out when their parts need replacing and book themselves in for a service. They can even detect mechanical faults and automatically inform a breakdown agency that a part is about to fail, when it will fail and where the car is likely to be at the time.

Seamless service

With a better understanding of customer needs, firms will also be able to re-engineer all their sales channels (in addition to their products and services). The aim is to align channels around the more clearly identified needs of different customer segments. A sales force, for example, could be divided and refocused on specific segments with clearly defined sales approaches aimed at the specific needs of customers in that segment. A business targeting a segment of working mothers might consider employing a sales team comprising women who have had children, for example.

Customers contacting a call centre, for example, could be sorted by customer segment, with pre-designed scripting for each segment. In the Triage stage the aim was to ensure that your golden 10% or 20% of customers received the best possible service while seemingly unprofitable customers were directed to a low cost response. But in the Integrate stage, firms can take a far more sophisticated approach.

For example, if customers have a greater opportunity to choose the product features they want before talking to a salesperson, that salesperson can spend more of his or her time closing the deal, rather than explaining unwanted options. The aim is to strike the most profitable balance between an automated response and the personal touch.

Likewise with branches, stores and other outlets. In the Triage stage, the aim is to cut costs and maximise effectiveness. In the Integrate stage, the value of these outlets is rethought and re-engineered. Bank branches, for example, are changed so that they reflect retail storefront best practices. Their very purpose should be reconsidered—they become places for friendly financial advice, rather than places to bank cheques and pay bills.

A similar change of approach applies to self-service channels, such as the Internet. In the Triage stage, use of self-service channels is encouraged as a means of cutting costs while giving good service. In the Integrate stage, they become a way of improving customer satisfaction and cross-selling other products and services. ATMs, for example, are transformed from being 'hole-in-the-wall' cash machines to sophisticated systems that can provide detailed information about your finances, allow you to pay bills and buy cinema tickets.

A key aim when transforming sales channels is to ensure that customers experience the organisation as a single entity. Why, for example, are customers passed from pillar to post when they approach their banks service provider with more than one query? Too often the right hand truly does not know what the left hand is doing.

This is symptomatic of a fundamental problem. Many

firms hold a wealth of detailed information about their customers, but they fail to use that information to either co-ordinate their marketing, sales and service initiatives, or to empower their staff to handle all of the issues that a single customer might raise with a member of staff. Firms need to overcome this structural handicap.

At this stage in the journey most firms are still fundamentally seller-driven. That means they are largely organised along product or channel lines, with each product or channel owner acting in a more-or-less uncoordinated way. As a consequence, they simply cannot address a customer's full requirements from one single point and their attempts to integrate products and sales channels into more attractive packages add costs that customers will not bear.

But as we move towards a buyer-driven world, organisations must offer a range of sales channels that work seamlessly to support a particular customer segment, rather than operating around simple product-specific channels. The customer must be able to deal with a co-ordinated, informed organisation, whether they access it through a storefront, a call centre, the Internet, or any other channel.

There is no easy way of becoming customer-centric, but here is my simple checklist of what a customer-centric firm must be able to do:

◆ Act as one unit even though it will consist of several.
◆ Learn something new from **each** customer interaction.
◆ Build a very comprehensive understanding of what each customer wants or might want and then let this knowledge drive their actions.
◆ Pleasantly surprise customers by the proactive action they take.

A number of firms have begun to make moves in this direction. American Express Financial Advisors (AEFA), for example, sells financial products such as insurance and mutual funds, and has recently reorganised itself with a focus on the way in which its staff sell its financial products. This has resulted in what initially looks like a return to values of the past, an emphasis on building relationships with customers rather than just making a sale to them.

In 1994 the Ford Motor Company made a widely publicised attempt to make its customer-services division more sensitive to the needs of customers. It tore up the old organisational chart with its functional responsibilities, and reorganised the 6,200-strong division around four key processes that it identified as creating customer satisfaction on the service side of the business. These were things like 'Fixing it right the first time, on time'. Ford got rid of the division's functional experts (on parts and marketing incentives, for example) in its desire to create greater overall customer satisfaction.

A director of the BOC Group, a UK producer of industrial gases, explained his company's reasons for restructuring its customer-services division:

We took the view that if we don't get the customer-service levels right, no matter what the cost, we'll have fewer customers to serve.

A firm that successfully navigates the Integrate stage will have begun to focus the organisation around the customer. But being customer-centric is not the same as being buyer-driven. There is still a heavy focus on push marketing. Most tellingly, while products and services are tailored to segments, they are not personalised to specific buyers.

Buyerise

The first two stages of our journey have been about cutting out dead wood and improving the way the firm does things. But let's not underestimate the challenge of successfully navigating the Triage and Integrate stages. For some firms, the changes they will need to make to get this far will be traumatic. We have seen already how some firms will struggle. Yet it is not until we reach the Buyerise stage that the scale of change required becomes fully apparent.

Here I am talking about nothing less than a revolutionary shift in the way that organisations do business. In this final stage, firms flip the paradigm, from seller-driven to buyer-driven. Basic principles about how to do business, which may well have worked successfully for decades, have to be reconsidered and, most likely, abandoned. Rather than aiming to offer 'solutions' to customer needs, firms need to go a step further and offer packages of products and services that meet a customer's fundamental 'intentions'. To achieve this firms will, most likely, have to form strategic alliances with organisations that can strengthen their hands and outsource key parts of the offering to these specialist providers.

Until the Buyerise stage, the challenge has been to group customers into segments, improve your under-standing of those segments and tailor your offerings to anticipated needs. In the Buyerise stage, firms face the challenge of treating *every* customer as an individual. That doesn't mean try being nicer to your customers in a smileas-they-enter-the-store 'have a nice day' kind of way. It means ensuring that both your dialogue with a customer as well as the products and services that you offer them are customised based on that *individual* customer's needs and desires.

In the Buyerise stage, strategies to win new customers become more fluid. Rather than relying on extensive research into consumer needs and segmentation, followed by lengthy product design and testing, strategy is created dynamically. Firms hypothesise about what consumers need or want and publicise their offering on the Internet. They then have to watch and learn—revising their offering as quickly as they can based on buyer response (or the lack of it).

In the Integrate stage, firms had to invest in systems that ensured that every time they had contact with a customer, anything that was said, done or assumed would be based on the most up-to-date information available about that customer. In the Buyerise stage, firms can reap the greater rewards of this investment.

A better understanding of individual customer needs can be built into each channel and contact-point so that the firm can have a personalised dialogue with every customer. At the same time, across every channel (whether automated or human) the firm will be able to make a highly personalised product or service offering based on the expressed preferences and behaviours of that *individual* customer.

For example, efforts to improve the effectiveness of the firm's sales force shift away from activity management and the perfection of standard scripts. Instead, you'll be striving to customise each and every dialogue that you have with each and every customer. This takes the firm far beyond simply automating sales tracking. The aim is to create what I call a 'Virtual Selling' process.

This process has five key elements:

1. A sales process that combines the best elements of automated and personal approaches so that sales staff can focus on closing deals.
2. Provision of rich customer and product information at point of sale.
3. Expert system-driven sales advice to customise product and selling approach based on specific customer profiles and transaction history.
4. Offload of routine administrative tasks to increase time for selling.
5. Seamless integration of sales management and sales reporting into the selling cycle.

Intentions marketing

Many of the innovative new firms that I have talked about in this book are achieving much of this already. Leading edge buyer-driven firms such as Intuit, Amazon.com and E*Trade are increasingly creating packaged solutions that include different types of products and services from different suppliers to meet the underlying comprehensive need that drives a purchase.

These firms are able to create these packaged offerings because they have forged strategic alliances with best-of-breed providers, rather than by trying to do everything in-house. This is what I call 'Intentions' marketing—selling to the broader underlying need.

Intuit's quicken.com site, for example, not only sells

Intuit software products, it is a comprehensive gateway to a wide variety of financial and non-financial needs, including mortgages, insurance, office supplies and a wide array of financial planning tools. In the same way, Amazon.com is going beyond selling books by offering, for example, adventure travel offers to those customers with an interest in adventure travel literature.

In addition, the line between sales and service delivery is becoming blurred. Effective buyer-driven firms draw upon usage patterns and customer profiles to transform service events into selling opportunities. For example, Yahoo! and Excite search engines display customised ads related to the search request—for example, type in a search for airfares and ads for specific airlines will be displayed along with the search results.

To compete with these buyer-driven firms, organisations need to evolve substantially both their business architectures (organisational structure, measurement systems etc.) and their technology architectures (applications, system hardware etc.). There are two key steps to achieving this.

First, they need to 'close the loop'. Most current approaches to data warehousing and data mining (the process of storing, analysing and sharing information) are seriously flawed. Too much attention is given to building giant-sized data banks and highly sophisticated analytical tools, while insufficient focus is put on establishing what I call a true 'closed loop' buyer-driven marketing process. The closed loop process differs from traditional direct marketing, which is all one-way, by:

✦ Closely tying all sales and service encounters into a common customer profile.

✦ Shaping the dialogue with the customer based on the customer profile.

✦ Recording the results of the interaction—whether successful or not.

Leading Internet firms such as Firefly are putting the closed-loop approach into practice. Firefly creates a customised profile based both on survey preferences and ongoing reaction to new offers to ensure that members are presented with offers tailored to them. Similarly, amazon.com will track likes and dislikes about books to alert members to new publications they should find appealing.

The second step is to create a buyer-driven architecture. Firms will have to face the problem that in a buyer-driven world some of the information they will want to feed into the customer profile will be controlled by the customer. They will only get access to this data if the prospective customer agrees. For example, the emerging P3P privacy protocol will allow users to set their desired level of privacy and negotiate exceptions. In addition, virtual sales agents are evolving that use customer profiles to sort through the range of competing offerings. These agents are likely to be both buyer-side agents and seller-side agents.

In this environment, the business architectures need to support both buyer- and seller-side information and agents. Faced with total information overload, consumers in the buyer-driven world will use intelligent agents to track down the best offerings to match their requirements. Firms need to ensure that they can make information available to these agents in a way that gets their offerings drawn to the attention of buyers. At the same time, when firms are making increasingly tailored and flexible offerings, employees will need to use intelligent agents that will collect information about consumer needs, prompt them about potentially attractive offerings and so on. Both these agents and profiles will work together to shape communication between consumers and businesses and to personalise the actual offering.

It's tough for old-established firms to adapt to this new world of intentions marketing. For it is a world that requires new attitudes to things like customer relationships and distribution channels. Firms will have to share customers and not set out to own them, and service-providers will have to reconsider their commitment to bricks-and-mortar and physical stores and outlets.

There are basically three routes available to large corporations which are hoping to enter the kingdom of intentions. The first is to leverage their existing products and services into the new networks that are beginning to be formed. The second is to aggregate their products and services with those of other (existing) industries and attempt to create a network of their own. And the third is to create an entirely new business for the purpose of forming networks and, ultimately, of satisfying customers' intentions.

Leveraging existing products and services into a nascent group requires a careful assessment of those products and services and an analysis of which intentions they might, in conjunction with others, come to satisfy. This is no easy task for an organisation that is tightly focused on its existing discrete products, and that is structured in a way to reflect that focus.

On the other hand, to try and create new networks with other established giant producers is undoubtedly the most difficult of the three strategies to follow. All parties to the network will have to undergo a fundamental shift in their mind-set—from one where they manufacture products for delivery to customers to one where they are part of a partnership focused on a group of people with common needs, needs which they (together with their partners) set out to satisfy.

Andersen Consulting's research suggests that the third option is the one most likely to be successful for existing large corporations. In this, traditional companies set up autonomous units that are independent of the old-style bureaucracy and central controls that can so easily stifle new in-house ventures.

These autonomous units will have to be run by the type of people who are suited to starting and running new businesses, and that excludes most of the traditional managers found in existing large organisations. They will need to have an entrepreneurial mentality and to foster the sort of innovative culture that is almost certainly alien to their parents.

The leaders of these units will almost certainly expect some sort of equity as part of a package of performance-related pay. And they will also have to be able to offer the same sort of package to others that they want to join their team.

The pace of change

The shift to a buyer-driven environment is fundamental. Firms need to both rapidly get their current business in order, aligning and integrating to meet customer needs, while preparing for an even more dramatic transformation.

Those that succeed will thrive, while the future for those who cannot transform is unattractive.

How long have our giants got to make these moves? The Triage stage should be completed as soon as possible— there is absolutely no time to spare. Yet some businesses will be able to stay in the Integrate stage for a long time. A few smart companies have realised that they don't have to try and shift their whole business to the buyer-driven model of stage three. It can make sense to keep the core business at the Integrate stage but to take part of it straight to step three by going '.com'.

By this I mean setting up a new online business with a new brand that has no visible link with the parent company. For example, in the banking sector. BankOne of the United States set up Wingspanbank.com to offer different products and services to a different segment of customers that, in the buyer-driven world, its regular business would find hard to reach. As the '.com' phenomenon gains pace, we may soon see the creation of several spin-off companies that are designed to handle different segments. The aim would be to use new online channels to go for different types of customer. Over time, that would gradually shrink the parent organisation and make the entire business increasingly virtual.

Ultimately, firms will need to choose how fast they want to move, and they will then have to accept the risk of having made the transition too slowly.

8

Conclusion

IT TOOK JUST ONE SECOND TO MOVE FROM THE LAST millennium into this new one. How can such an arbitrary event have any real impact on a business? Assuming that a firm dealt with its Y2K exposure in good time, the return to work after the New Year break should have been just another day at the office. Well, to an extent it was just like any other day. In many ways nothing has changed at all. But in more important ways, everything is different.

The forces of change I have described in this book achieved an unstoppable momentum at the end of the last millennium. But the pressures on our business giants have been growing for many years. That is why, in a sense, nothing has changed. The challenge facing business leaders is becoming increasingly clear, and I hope that this book will make it clearer still. But the challenge is the same as it was on 31 December 1999. (See Figure 8.1).

But it's also true that everything is completely different. To thrive in the buyer-driven world, businesses will need to rethink everything that they do. But fears about Y2K compliance caused many firms to put their brains in neutral while they worried about the countdown to the millennium. Now that we have passed that artificial barrier, they are ready to start thinking again. Having spent far too long looking inwards, these firms are in for a shock.

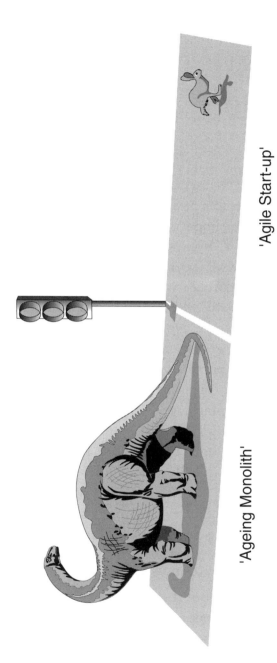

'Agile Start-up'

'Ageing Monolith'

Figure 8.1   Act now . . . or get left behind

Customers in control

Small, innovative firms that did not have old, bug-riddled computer systems have been stealing their markets. These companies were able to start from scratch with new systems that were already Y2K safe. But more importantly, they have created startling new ways of doing business built around innovative technologies and a smarter understanding of how the world is going to work in future.

The leaders of these firms know that (at best) big businesses will find it tough to meet the new demands of empowered, 'wised-up' consumers and that (at worst) people don't want to do business with giant firms anymore. And this isn't just a change affecting developed western economies. In 1987, the Chinese Consumer Association received just 150 letters of complaint from dissatisfied shoppers. Now it gets well over half a million a year, mostly about poor service.

The new market entrants that pose the greatest threat are usually small companies that focus on one product or service, one customer segment and one market channel. They are everything that our giants are not. Life will be tough for the chief executives trying to recover lost ground. It'll be like trying to swat flies with a sledgehammer or catching a speedboat with a super-tanker. Unless they change the way they think about their businesses and address some fundamental challenges, they don't stand much of a chance.

I am not predicting the imminent demise of all giant firms. As I have shown in earlier chapters, some leading big businesses have started to experiment with the right kind of changes. We have already seen the launch of EGG from the

Prudential insurance company, a service which gives customers some ability to design their own products. Other similar ventures are in the pipeline, encouraged by the market's valuation of the EGG business at £3.6 billion after only a few short months in business.

Act now . . .

But having said that, **there is no time for delay**. The buyer-driven world gets nearer every day. I constantly see signs of its rapid emergence, of firms becoming more customer-centric, moving away from commodity products and outsourcing as much as they can.

Mondus.com, for example, claims to be the world's first online business-to-business marketplace where small businesses put their purchasing needs out for bid, and suppliers have the opportunity to submit detailed proposals to them. The company is based in Oxford, England—but it's focusing its initial marketing efforts on the United States and Germany as well as the UK. This company is global from day one.

priceline.com became one of the world's 10 most-visited eCommerce sites just six weeks after its launch. In its first 120 days, the site sold more than 40,000 airline tickets, making priceline.com one of the 10 largest sellers of leisure airline tickets in the United States. The company behind priceline.com has now been issued with a patent protecting both the broad concepts and key functionality of its buyer-driven commerce model. It is also said to have another 250 patent applications pending.

. . . Or get left behind

Everyone involved in business life needs to think about their role in the buyer-driven future. Personally, I started writing this book as a senior partner with Andersen Consulting and ended it as the CEO of my own start-up company, @speed.

The firms and individuals that will thrive are those that move quickly, get ahead and stay ahead. In any type of business, a firm that once dominated a market can lose its way. In the UK, for example, Marks & Spencer used to be synonymous with dependable, value clothing for women who want to be smart and sensibly fashionable. Then a bureaucratic buying structure and some bad choices left it out of touch with its core constituency. Rival firms rapidly caught up and M&S is working hard to put things right. But when you're running a buyer-driven business and your main sales channel is the Internet, you don't get a second chance to meet customer needs.

In the hot-house environment of Internet start-ups, product design cycles shrink from years to months. Nobody has any time-to-market advantage because any new product, service, benefit or feature can be copied or bettered in 24 hours. This is a world where being first is everything, where a 23-year-old entrepreneur can raise $50 million to launch a loss-making eCommerce business with a six-month exit strategy.

Move within the cube

The cube that I have described is a way of thinking about the challenge of transforming a seller-driven, product-focused organisation that does everything in-house into a buyer-driven, intentions-focused 'virtual' organisation. There are plenty of examples of firms attempting to work their way through the cube along my preferred path, the three-stage transition of Triage, Integrate and Buyerise.

Not every organisation will finish the journey intact, but not every organisation needs to. The increased pressure to outsource non-core areas, develop strategic alliances and focus on core competencies will cause many big firms to disintegrate. But that is no bad thing. The trick is in knowing what your core competencies *really* are, forming strategic alliances with the *right* people and so on.

In essence, it's about knowing how far you need to go towards being a buyer-driven, virtual enterprise—knowing how you plan to get to *your chosen* destination. You might make some wrong choices, but a failure to address these issues *immediately* is a luxury no firm can afford. Unless you can change your organisation so that it can compete with a new market entrant built on a completely different and more effective economic model, you will be beaten.

Can your organisation *be* changed to that extent? When I first started working on this book I had a meeting with the head of a well-known UK building society. He gazed thoughtfully out of his office window at the vacant lot opposite. 'I think I might have to buy that land', he told me. 'Why?' I asked him. 'The prospect of changing this organisation is so daunting that I might just decide to demolish the whole lot and rebuild it the way I want it right over there', he said. Tellingly, the new site was far smaller.

Desperate times do indeed call for desperate measures.

But for those of you merely looking for some sensible ways forward, I hope this book has helped you find some.

The thing to remember above all else? Simply, that it's time to change. Now.

Index